Stop Cybercrime from Ruining *Your* Life!

Sixty Secrets to Keep You Safe

CYNTHIA JAMES

CERTIFIED INFORMATION SYSTEMS
SECURITY PROFESSIONAL (CISSP)

ISBN: 0615789714
ISBN-13: 9780615789712

Library of Congress Control Number: 2013936692, Stray Cat Press, Los Gatos, Ca

First Edition

Stray Cat Press
www.straycatpress.com

For information about permission to reproduce selections from this book, write to
Permissions, Stray Cat Press, 15466 Los Gatos Blvd #109-212
Los Gatos, CA 95032

DEDICATION

To Nick and Matt – my two best reasons for doing anything.

Love,
Mom

ACKNOWLEDGMENTS

I could not have finished this book without the incredible support of my best writing buddy Deb Atwood. May our marvelous El Cheapo Writing retreats continue as long as we do. I'm grateful as well for the superb assistance of my editor and friend Meera Lester, and for the time both my father, Capt. Edmund Melvin (USN, ret.) and my cousin David Melvin generously applied to correcting typos in the first edition. A special thank you also goes to my boss and friend Alexander Karpitsky who took the time to preview my early manuscript and to comment. Finally, without Kaspersky Lab and the tremendous people working there – including the marvelous example set by Eugene Kaspersky – I surely would not have developed such a passion for this fascinating subject of cybersecurity in the first place.

TABLE OF CONTENTS

INTRODUCTION:

Beating the Cybercrime Bear

What if you saw the following advertisement from an employer?

Seeking English-speaking employees for three weeks of semi-nefarious activity. Earn up to $1,000,000. All computer proficient applicants will be considered, hacker tools provided, minor risk of prosecution.

Of course, you might doubt the number of zeros involved, but let's suppose the employer could prove the dollar amount was legitimate. Does it sound like a tempting offer? Better yet, what if the activity wasn't illegal? Would you presume there would be millions of applicants?

Cybercrime **does** pay this well, which is how it attracts some of the best and brightest minds in the world. Cybercriminals can earn $2 million in just 24 hours of running a good scam – or, in two recent examples, $33 million over nine months and $14 million in 48 hours. Although distributing malware and hacking into private networks is illegal in the United States, in many other countries it's not. Or, even if technically it **is** illegal, it's rarely prosecuted.

This is why the problem of **cybercrime will never go away.** Profits are high, risks are low, and in many countries, other employment options are scarce.

These huge profits are being used to hire the best possible writers (have you noticed how clever some spam has become?) and to engineer more effective attacks. In fact, a majority of cybercrime attacks have become completely invisible: commonly, people have no idea *when* they are being attacked and infected. An estimated 50 million personal computers (PCs) and laptops worldwide today **are under the control of hackers, while PC owners have no idea an infection has occurred**. This is because cybercriminal techniques for sneaking malicious code onto our computers become more clever every day.[1] Hackers keep getting better while PC owners plod along in ignorant bliss.

Once a hacker's code is living on your system, he can see every key stroke you make. This includes the log in information and passwords for every website you visit. The hacker may also rent the use of your computer to other people, or use your computer to launch more attacks. He will try to quietly infect everyone else you know. If you have any financial assets, he will steal those along with your identity. Meanwhile you won't even know you were infected until the day you realize your bank accounts are empty and your credit is ruined. It's an expensive and time-consuming mess to clean up.

As harsh as all this sounds, when it comes to cybercriminals and their tactics, there is some good news. Once you know what they are up to, it's *not* impossible to defend yourself against their activities and you don't have to be a computer whiz to outsmart them. Just follow the rules in this easy-to-implement book.

In fact, by following a few basic rules you'll be safer than 75% of the people you know. Follow a few more and you'll reach the 90% range. If you are willing to accept the Cybersecurity Fitness Challenge, you can be 300% safer than the average, non-technical user within a week. That challenge is simply: *Devote 10 minutes a day towards implementing the strategies in this book and do it for 10 days.*

---

1 "Malicious software" is also called malware for short, so these terms are interchangeable.

Have you heard the joke about the two guys and the bear?

Joe and Mark are camping in the woods. They awaken to a commotion and scramble out of their tent to see a huge, angry looking bear lumbering towards them. Joe grabs his running shoes and frantically starts jamming his feet into them. His friend Mark yells, "Why the heck would you do that now? We have to outrun the bear!" And Joe says, "Actually, no—I only have to outrun you."

Cybercriminals are a lot like bears. They don't really care if it's Mark or Joe, they're happy to eat whichever one they catch first. So if you're even just a little bit harder to attack than the next mark, you may succeed in outrunning the bear for at least another day.

CHAPTER 1

Why Worry? – What's *Really* at Stake

FACT BOX: Cybercriminals earn billions of dollars a year. What used to be an activity for teenage hackers (who mostly got their kicks from making headlines) has turned into a serious livelihood for many thousands of people worldwide. Between 2004 and 2012, malicious attack software circulating on the Internet went from approximately 200,000 unique pieces per year to over 50 million per year. This translated into over 1.5 billion cybercrime attacks. The actual *cash* lost by victims worldwide in 2012 was estimated to be over $100 billion.[1]

Cybercrime has grown astronomically since 2005. The Internet, with its billions of connected devices, provides many more potential victims than even the largest city does. And many easily-hacked companies are holding personal details about us which cybercriminals can use to defraud us. Whether it's a cyberpredator stalking his or her prey, an old-fashioned bank robber, or a cat burglar, criminals of nearly every type can increase their odds of success by adding an Internet component to their crime.

WHAT THE EXPERTS THINK

Even for experts, cybercrime is not an easy problem to solve. There are now many companies in the world – such as the one

---

1 Here are two studies by cybersecurity companies: http://www.securelist.com/en/analysis/204792255/ Kaspersky_Security_Bulletin_2012_The_overall_statistics_for_2012 ; and http://www.symantec.com/ about/news/release/article.jsp?prid=20120905_02 ;

I work for – that offer specialized anti-cybercrime solutions for many different types of cybercrime attacks. These business "opportunities" only exist because the rate of cybercrime is increasing so rapidly.

One of the biggest challenges for cybercrime fighters is that a lot of the work we do to protect users from malware can be seen by cybercriminals. Every day we download tiny bits of code called "signatures" to a protected computer. These will recognize and block the latest malware. If cybercriminals want to test new malware, they can purchase our anti-virus software and test it against those signatures. They will also be able to see the new anti-malware updates as they come in, and the criminals will know when we have blocked certain types of threats but not others. Consequently, we are always at a disadvantage. We do the best we can as quickly as possible to defeat their latest tricks, but make no mistake: it's a hard job, and it easily absorbs all the resources we commit to it.

HOW THEY TRICK US

Cybercriminals will do anything – and masquerade as anyone – to get what they want. They will send email that is variously warm, flattering, familiar, or threatening. They will ask us to accept a prize, or pay taxes on a boat we don't own, or agree to be listed in a prestigious directory. Their goal is to get us to react by opening an infected file or clicking on a link to an infected website. Most often, we never know what hit us.

An email arrives from the Internal Revenue Service demanding that you pay taxes on your Ferrari – except you don't own one. Before you stop to consider why Uncle Sam is only reaching out by email, curiosity gets the better of you and you click on the link. The website *does* have an IRS logo. It *looks* legitimate. Come to think of it, the email from United Parcel Service (UPS) looks real too, and it comes with shipping details attached. Naturally, you'd like to know what someone has sent you. You open the attached file to find out.

But you've been duped: both emails are from cybercriminals. When possible, they will copy legitimate email word-for-word, and it will come bearing the official logo of the company or organization they are pretending to be. Whether the mistake you made was connecting to an infected website or opening an infected file, without so much as a hello, a nasty little virus has snuck onto your hard drive.[2] Or, it slipped quietly onto your smartphone. Meanwhile, you're still trying to figure out why Uncle Sam thinks you're so rich and why UPS sent you such gibberish.

A virus like the one you now have is smarter than most people. It's also an obedient little trooper, capable of reaching out to its leader (called a "bot-herder" because he manages a network of compromised PCs called "bots") and getting instructions. Those instructions could be:

"Watch every move Ms. Clueless makes. When she opens a banking website, record every keystroke. In the middle of the night, wake up and send me those user names and passwords. Erase your tracks. Go back to sleep."

Or, maybe the instructions are:

"Wait until Mr. Oblivious is asleep. Wake up. Send email to everyone in his address book with links to more viruses. Erase your tracks. Go back to sleep."

Sometimes this smart little virus even tells its boss how much money you have in your account. This saves the bot-herder some time, because he doesn't want to bother with less than $1,000. He especially likes to prioritize accounts over $5,000. He hands over these leads to his staff of hackers so they can siphon out your money, and he leaves Kazakhstan to party in Paris. If the virus got your credit card numbers too, he'll rent a Ferrari while he's there.

---

2 For the purposes of this book, I'll use the word "virus" and "malware" (short for malicious software) interchangeably although it's not strictly correct. But at the introductory level there's not very much benefit in explaining the distinctions security geeks make between Trojans, worms and viruses, all of which are considered "malware."

There is a saying in the security industry: "It's not a matter of **if** you will be compromised or stolen from, it's only a matter of **when.**"[3]

WHAT MOTIVATES THEM

The preceding scenario describes the behavior of a garden variety piece of malware and its owner, the cybercriminal. In such a case, the cybercriminal is in it for the money. You can find out more about how he does his job in the next chapter. But before we move on, there's another more disgusting group we need to talk about: Cyber-Sickos. Cops also call them "Internet Predators."

Unfortunately, the same rocking connectivity that provides you with email and helps you locate the only beekeeper in Antarctica has also made it easier for psycho-losers to hunt their human prey.[4] Personal blogs, social networking sites, and public records are just a few of the sources they use. Whether the data consists of photographs or financial records, and whether it's posted for the public or limited to friends, if it touches the Internet your data can always be hacked. And these days, every school, every company, and most government agencies are connected to the Internet somewhere, somehow.[4]

HACKING NOT REQUIRED

Sometimes the information we share practically invites catastrophe. A reporter for *Time Magazine,* Graeme McMillan, wrote:

> "Next time you leave your home for any appreciable length of time, whatever you do, *don't tell the Internet.* A new study has revealed that an unsettling 78% of burglars use social media such as Twitter, Facebook and Foursquare to choose where they're going to break in next."[5]

---

3 When a cybercriminal breaks through security precautions we call it a "breach".
4 More about these perverts in Chapter 6.
5 http://techland.time.com/2011/09/27/burglars-now-using-twitter-facebook-against-you/ for Graeme's article; http://www.mediabistro.com/alltwitter/social-burglars_b14237 for the original study.

The study McMillan is referring to, where security professionals interviewed convicted burglars about the digital tools they use, also revealed that they used Google Street View to help plan the attack.

Since that article was published, technology has taken an even more profitable twist for burglars: photos taken by smart phones have geolocation tags (longitude and latitude coordinates) embedded in them.[6] Anyone can download the free software to read these. A photo that a child posts or circulates of the new trampoline in the backyard, combined with information about an upcoming trip, has just made his or her house a target.

TOO MUCH INFORMATION

Here are some other ways in which the sharing of too much information over the Internet can get us into trouble:

- Increasingly, employers check social media as part of the hiring process. They are looking for red flags which indicate ethical or legal issues. *That picture of your friend joking around with drug paraphernalia – or even your mention of the co-worker you used to date – is all it takes to nix an offer letter.*

- In January of 2013, on the MediaBistro website, Mary Long wrote about teenagers coming back to school after the holidays. Many of them were tweeting variations of the message, "if someone wants to blow up the school before tomorrow, that would be awesome".[7] The FBI arrested a teen who took it one step further: "Does anyone want to help me blow up the school?" The subtitle of Mary's article is: "Do you know what YOUR little angel is tweeting on Twitter?"

- Guess what the convergence of these three trends means:

---

6 See Appendix F for information on how to turn this feature off.
7 http://www.mediabistro.com/alltwitter/teen-arrested-for-terroristic-tweets_b33943

- o A smartphone's ability to record footage anywhere and anytime

- o More surveillance cameras than ever before *everywhere* as wireless Webcams become cheaper

- o The simplicity of uploading clips to YouTube

That's right! The potential for suffering everlasting embarrassment is higher than it has been in the history of humankind. Anything which can publicly embarrass us also exposes us to security risks. It's not hard to figure out where a lot of footage was taken, and technology like face-matching software has made it easier than ever for cybercriminals to find us - *and* our charming children.

THREATS POSED BY CONNECTION MANIA

Twitter has provided some people the equivalent of an intravenous drip connected directly to their brains. Even the most "fad-resistant" among us are increasingly more addicted to devices with constant, full-time Internet connections. At this point, there's little hope of recovery, simply because it's so darn fun. Worldwide, there are now more Internet-connected mobile devices than there are human beings![8] And:

"By 2015 there will be an average of 5.8 Internet-connected devices per person in North America..."[9]

We all love the convenience and excitement of having the world at our fingertips. But every new Internet device adds risk, since the easiest way to infect a system is via the Internet. An infection by malicious software – called "malware" for short – means data loss, and data loss can lead to financial loss.

---

8 According to Cisco: http://arstechnica.com/business/2012/02/mobile-internet-devices-will-outnumber-humans-this-year-cisco-predicts/
9 Statistic provided to Mashable by Cisco: http://mashable.com/2011/06/09/global-internet-traffic-infographic/

Even if we decide to shun technology altogether and head to a cabin in the woods, or keep only one "dumb" cell phone for the rest of our lives, we can't keep our friends and family from treading on the bleeding edge. And as long as they're still exchanging emails and texts with us, we're getting dragged along too.

IT'S NOT JUST ABOUT YOU

Who else has our social security numbers and addresses? Where else on the Internet do our identities "live"? When an entity that has your data gets hacked, the result may be expensive and inconvenient. But we can't entirely eliminate this risk. If we want to live happily – which for most people includes online banking, shopping, and paying bills not to mention receiving news, email, and updates – we are unfortunately forced to trust at least some of the following entities with our information:

- banks and credit card companies
- services to which we subscribe
- online department stores
- hospitals
- insurance companies
- travel agencies
- government agencies
- employer 401K accounts
- educational institutions

I like to call these guys "Butterballs", because they are frequently stuffed with more data than they need, they are always asking for more, and they are constantly under attack by hungry cybercriminals.[10] One scary thing about a Butterball is that it also prefers to stay as quiet as possible about a data breach, so often we don't even know our data has been stolen.[11] And in this analogy,

---

10 A Butterball is also the trademarked name of a line of turkeys.
11 An example of state law regarding data breaches warns against "unreasonable delay" in notifying customers their data has been stolen, but stops short of specifying how long is "unreasonable" http://www.leginfo.ca.gov/cgi-bin/displaycode?section=civ&group=01001-02000&file=1798.80-1798.84

cybercriminals are such gluttons that the attacks are relentless. But we can't wish away these holders-of-our-data; Butterballs are a necessary evil. What's important is to acknowledge the risk they represent and find ways to reduce it. In fact, there is a comprehensive list of rules and suggestions for managing interaction with Butterballs in Chapter 5.

SAFETY FOR THE VILLAGE

There's one last important piece of calculating your personal vulnerability. It was succinctly summed up by John Donne with the phrase, "no man [or woman] is an island." Presuming you have some friends and/or family, here are some potential consequences of cybercrime which you may not have considered:

a.) Dear Aunt Mildred loses her life savings to an online Lothario. She calls to ask – tearfully – if she can move in with you.

b.) Your nephew's entire college fund disappears overnight. The bankers claim it's not their fault since his father's computer was hacked.

c.) The $52,000 raised by your son's high school (mostly through the efforts of parents) disappeared in one fell swoop because the district bank account was hacked. Since the money has already been transferred out of the country, there's nothing that can be done. Your son's water polo team won't be getting a new pool this year after all.

The point here is that even if you are perfectly able to take care of yourself, unless you share Internet safety information with people or groups you care about, you will still suffer. So begin making a list of the people who populate your Village now. The appendixes are created to be easily shared with others so please share them freely.

HELPING YOU STAY SAFE

Navigating safely through Internet waters isn't very hard, but it does require the guidance of a person you trust. That should be someone who has broad knowledge of security, since successful cybercrime often involves the coordinated breaching of software, hardware, and even physical locations of data. Ideally it is also someone who is active in the cybersecurity industry with access to the latest cybercrime tactics and anti-cybercrime solutions. This is where I come in – and here are some reasons I believe I can help.

First, I do have this nifty security certification called a CISSP which requires an understanding of security across 10 different security domains.[12] This means that in addition to basic hacking techniques, I have a good grasp of how cybercriminals can manipulate physical security and use social engineering and encryption methods to steal the data they want.[13]

Second, I constantly work with intense, narrowly focused, mega-geeks who are completely dedicated to anti-cybercrime. Our company employs experts on mobile threats, experts on botnet discovery, and experts on forensics (the scientific analysis of the cybercrime scene, after the fact). Because anti-cybercrime companies such as mine are often the first ones in the world to discover the latest cybercrime scams, we work with everyone from consumers to government agencies to major corporations. This gives us a very broad and in-depth perspective on malware.

Third, I spend a lot of my time simplifying the latest cybercrime information for audiences who want to be safer. I translate such data for consumption by non-geeks. For example, I recently perused a 20-page technical paper (called a "threat *brief*", how funny) about the way a particular threat operates. On page 16, the author mentioned two policies which should be changed to thwart such future attacks. Since this kind of attack will soon be copied and turned against consumers and their Butterballs, everyone

---

12 Certified Information Systems Security Professional.
13 "Social engineering" is just a fancy way of saying, "when people are conned."

needs these tips. But you have a life, right? You don't have time for ridiculously lengthy briefs of narrow focus, do you? I know what you mean; if it wasn't my job, I wouldn't either. But it is, and so I do.

HOW TO USE THIS BOOK

If you want to learn it all, including how cybercriminals turn *your* data into *their* money and why they are so successful at fooling us, start at the beginning. If you're too freaked out to wait, go straight to the Cybercrime Sixty safety rules in the appendixes. Implement the rules immediately, then return to earlier chapters if you'd like to know why they are important.

STAYING UP TO DATE

It's very important in the area of Internet safety to stay informed. No one in security can know it all, but you should be able to find solid sources to provide you with the most critical Internet safety news. I blog about recent news and threats at www.cynthiajames. com, aka www.cjonsecurity.com. You can also find all the web resources and informational links which are in this book at my website. Speaking of which, the Federal Bureau of Investigation (FBI) maintains a website which issues "cyber alerts" whenever it believes a threat has reached a certain danger threshold – for example, to warn potential victims when a successful multi-million dollar scam has really taken off, or a particularly malicious cyber-predator is operating. You can find the link to the FBI's website in appendix F along with numerous other helpful links and suggested publications and ezines. So subscribe to a blog you enjoy and consider following your favorite "consumer security" experts on twitter.

CHAPTER 2

Our Love Affair with the Internet –
For Better or For Worse

FACT BOX: While addressing the graduating class of Boston University students in 2012, the CEO of Google, Eric Schmidt, implored them to "take one hour a day and turn that thing [Internet and phone connectivity] off." He suggested that instead they "have a real conversation" with someone they love. But he also said that this generation of students is more equipped than any generation before them to make history because of their technical prowess. "Connectivity will revolutionize every aspect of society — politically, socially, economically," he said. "To connect the world is to free the world."

In Chapter 1 we talked about how much we all use the Internet. But we didn't address the question: Why not just stop? There are still some people in the world today who think this may be possible. But it's not. In order to fully grasp the current situation, let's go back in time a bit since it's always hard to be objective about the era in which we live.

WAY BACK WHEN

Once upon a time, books were more precious than gold. That was because there was no way to mass-produce them. One book could easily take more than a year to create – and that was with a scribe working at it full time. In addition to a scribe, we would need a narrator. If these roles were filled by the same person, less than 1% of the population would be capable of producing a book. The author would also have to purchase some sort of very durable material to write the book on, which was expensive. Otherwise the book would disintegrate too soon (the oldest existing book in the world today is 2,500 years old and is written on pages of 24-carat gold).[1]

Thus, way back then – in the Dark Ages[2] – there was no reliable way to mass-distribute ideas and information. The vast amount of expertise, information, and stories that human beings were capable of creating was not:

1.) Accumulated or protected (the loss of a race or a tribe meant the loss of all their knowledge)

2.) Easily and accurately spread across generations or across geographies (except verbally)

3.) Casually consumed – most people were not literate, and books certainly weren't disposable (they were heavily safeguarded, not the sort of thing to toss into the camel pack for a weekend getaway)

For the average person, all information in those days was spread via word-of-mouth which, as anyone who has played the game of Telephone[3] knows, is worse than a celebrity tabloid (in terms of accuracy). Also, without a basis for sharing ideas across large groups of people, there was much less opportunity for innovation.[4]

---

1 Held by Bulgaria's National Museum of History: six pages of beaten 24-carat gold.
2 Actually it was what we now call the "Early Middle Ages" – historians no longer use the term Dark Ages . But it's quite appropriate in this context as the time during which there were very few books!
3 This is the game where a circle of people whisper a phrase to each other one by one to see how many errors show up in the final version.
4 There were no "shoulders of giants to stand on," as Isaac Newton said (a phrase he attributed to Bernard of Chartres).

ALONG CAME...A PRINTING PRESS

Then Johann Gutenberg came along in 1455 and created the first printing press. In semi-automated fashion he could print lots of pages and many copies relatively quickly.[5] His ideas spread across multiple continents and they were improved upon. The Renaissance followed, along with giant leaps forward in science and a wider distribution of religion. Thus, the mass production of books – and the dissemination of information it allowed - revolutionized the world.[6]

The Internet - for all the aggravation it brings with it, much of it security-related - is no less of monumental step forward for humankind. Even if we wanted to, we don't have the power to wish that away.

A TOOL FOR AN IMPROVED WORLD

In many ways, what books have been accomplishing for humankind for the last five hundred years, the Internet suddenly is able to do *much better* today. This includes at least:

- **Education** – offers a staggering quantity of material online

- **Accessibility** – provides easy surfing–all it takes is wi-fi (wireless fidelity) and an Internet device

- **Useful information** – searches how to fix, feed, manage, raise, cook or kill just about anything

- **Entertainment** – caters to every taste

- **Exposed secrets and lies** – facilitates transparency (the job of an evil dictator is harder every day!)

---

5 Even though Gutenberg's first books sold for the equivalent of 3 years' salary, his invention continued to be refined until it resulted in modern printing.

6 The first newspapers – disposable documents for the public! – came along about a 150 years later.

All of this is great, right? And the Internet does each of these things better than printed media ever has:

- It's cheaper.
- Easier to transport.
- Data reaches us much faster than ever before.

The only bummer with all this is that cybercrime rides the same wave as the data that flows into our homes, schools, businesses, and pocketbooks. In fact, usage of the Internet and the increase of cybercrime have occurred on perfectly parallel tracks. Let's look at how quickly the internet has grown as this will give us a sense for how much more change – and security challenge – to expect in the future:

- Tim Berners-Lee first coined the term "World Wide Web" in 1990 [7]

- In the year **2000, there were 361million** people on the Internet worldwide

- As of **2012 there were over 2.3 billion** people on the Internet worldwide

So in just over 10 years, more than one-third of the world has jumped onto the Internet. [8]

INTERNET LOVE – AND POWER

The reason for this, of course, is that there are huge payoffs for connecting. It's fun, entertaining, educational, and socially invigorating. [9] In addition, it provides access to all kinds of necessities, conveniences, and luxuries to help us better enjoy our lives, including online shopping, scheduling, and mapping (to

---

7 I like Mike Cherim's timeline on this because it shows how many ideas had to come together to make www possible: http://green-beast.com/blog/?p=124

8 By comparison, it took closer to 400 years for books to become relatively commonplace.

9 It also enables revolutions, not of such personal interest to North American audiences but definitely a driver of adoption in many parts of the world.

name a few). Critical "infrastructure" organizations rely on it too – law enforcement, hospitals, universities, and government agencies.

The Internet has also become a critical business tool, which most businesses depend upon. Internet shopping increases by 10% a year on average. Many projections conclude that by 2015 the *majority* of our shopping will be done via Internet.

At this point, the Internet has the momentum of a bullet train speeding through an ever-expanding universe. We can forget about ever stopping the train. It is well-fueled by our thirst for information, quest for convenience, and appetite for connection. Like indoor plumbing, heating systems, and books – we're never going back. At a personal level, the Internet has become integral to our quality of life. In terms of the larger perspective, it has become integral to how we are evolving – and solving problems – as a species. Unfortunately, a certain number of seats on the cybertrain are taken up by criminals. Like rats, they are the inevitable parasites that come with cargo. If we can't eliminate them, we must find ways to tolerate them without sustaining too much damage.

PERSONAL INFORMATION LEAKAGE

In Chapter 1, we talked about the 5.8 devices that soon we all will have (resistance is futile!). Anyone who doesn't believe that this will happen to him or her simply hasn't discovered the latest and greatest invention. Every day new ingenious applications and products are hitting the market – things we never thought about connecting to the Internet which make our lives richer. It's not long before we believe that we could never have lived without them. Whether we are shoppers, gamers, or hobbyists – these devices are coming. Let's just take the high-tech pollsters word for it.

Internet fun is a great thing. But it has a major security flaw: the flow of data goes both ways. If we aren't careful, our households begin leaking out huge amounts of personal data. Even for people who believe in "radical visibility," there is plenty to worry about.[10] Once hackers can see our data, we may as well live in a glass house. They will profit from any of our information useful to them, and they will gladly sell what they can't use to other criminals.

Remember the Butterballs we talked about in Chapter1? Butterballs are all the companies out there that have accumulated way too much information about us. What if they have leaky pipes too? Is there anything we can do about that? Butterballs are much more likely to be targeted by hungry cybercriminals than any individual user is, since they have vast numbers of valuable records on people like us.

BAD NEWS, GOOD NEWS

The bad news is that there are no super-heroes to save us in this fight. No Mr. Incredible or Big Brother (aka the U. S. government) or any single security device. Even if they wanted to rescue us, they can't. They can help a little bit (see the Good News, Part One below), but the cybercrime problem is just too spread out, too well-financed, too easy to get into, and too segmented for these good guys to conquer it. Cybercriminals are parasites who continue to multiply on a vigorously growing host. And the host was designed with a weakness for these parasites because the Internet:

- Is a trusted network

- Protects our anonymity (to a large degree)

- Allows virtually anyone with a computing device to enter

Unless you kill the host, these happy little parasites aren't going anywhere.

---

10 Radical visibility is the idea that if all data everywhere were shared or known, we could all make better decisions about everything.

THE SECURITY TRADEOFF

Here's something rather obvious that even security professionals sometimes forget. We can get so wrapped up in adding more security that we forget that the ultimate security solution really isn't very difficult. "Perfect Security" keeps everything from the outside from getting in and everything from the inside from going out. By example, if you want perfect security for your home, put up a 30-foot fence, add barb wire to the top, electrify it, and don't let anyone in or out. It's hardly an impossible problem to solve.

But, of course, no one wants to live that way, without friends, fun and shopping. Likewise, the Internet gives us stimulation, collaboration, connectivity, and convenience. These occur to a large degree because of the freedom people have to browse, shop, and share ideas. The problem we are really trying to solve is this: how do we keep this marvelous network alive and thriving, with all its inflow and outflow, and *still* protect ourselves?

THE GOOD NEWS, PART ONE

Although no one can solve the problem completely, we aren't entirely alone either. For example, there are whole companies committed to fighting malware around the clock, year after year. All of us should already be using at least one of these software products (anti-virus or anti-malware for PCs, Macs, and cell phones). But that's not enough. We all need some basic education on the issues. And we all need to be updated on tactics once a year if we want to avoid the latest cyber scams.

THE GOOD NEWS, PART TWO

There's one other fact which everyone in security knows. And while it's bad news for business, it actually turns out to be pretty good news for individuals. That is this: **the weakest link in the security chain is the human being.** A huge majority of data breaches and monetary thefts are set in motion by employees who *know* they are breaking the rules. Joe Smith just couldn't resist the link that should have taken him to the best Viagra deal ever or heck, maybe that porn link his friend sent him really is a "clean" site after all. Everyone else is at lunch - can it really hurt to check it out? Not to pick on guys; they aren't the only ones who break the rules. Female employees do silly things too, just maybe not the same silly things.

In fact, if it sounds like we private citizens have it tough, consider the headache of running a 100 employee company. One mistake by one person and suddenly the company has $500,000 less in the bank: Ouch! A high price to pay for a little online shopping. And these are relatively **honest** mistakes. What about the angry employee who got passed over for a raise but has access to data which cybercriminals will pay for? Or, the employee who was fired but never was taken off the list of privileged users? These are some of the things that keep upper management awake at night. At least, we hope it does – especially if they happen to have our credit card data in their networks. (We talk about which rules to follow at work in Chapter 10.) Infection is also able to cross over from a work network to a home computer, so it really matters to all of us that our co-workers behave themselves.

But back to why it is good news for us that human behavior poses the highest risk: **if we're willing to follow just a few basic safety rules, and get others in our household to do the same** (which doesn't mean we can't have fun, by the way) **we will eliminate the largest amount of risk.**

In fact, anyone who will devote even 10 minutes a day can be 300% safer within a week. And the very *best* part of all this? Since changes in behavior provide the most dramatic improvements in our internet safety, except for an investment in this book, peace of mind may not cost a thing. In the next chapter, we'll talk about how cybercriminals operate and learn a little bit about how infections occur.

CHAPTER 3

How Hacker Hal Takes Control - of *Your* System

FACT BOX: In December of 2012, the FBI arrested 10 people who were responsible for infecting over 11 million computers and caused more than $850 million in losses over two years. Facebook assisted the FBI by identifying victims and suspects after their users were targeted by this group in 2010.

HISTORICALLY: HACKERS AT LARGE

Back in the late 1990s, people who created viruses were mostly teens or socially stunted grown-ups. They were geeks with a penchant for mayhem or a thirst for notoriety and nothing better to do over a weekend than try to break into someone's system or network. They would set up an auto-dialer to call random numbers until it received data feedback. When the auto dialer connected to someone's modem, the geeks would try to hack into the computer or network on the other end.

The hackers might even try putting together some malicious new code (these days we call malicious software "malware") and send it out via email to strangers. Their hacking goals were simple – mostly fun and games, because there was no real profit in doing it back then. Not enough people were banking over the Internet, and there was no organized market where they could sell credit card numbers if they succeeded in stealing any. To make money off stolen card numbers, a hacker would have to move far beyond his area of expertise and either sell them or try to use them himself (or herself, but there weren't many women doing it). Hackers knew they were causing mayhem but for the most part they didn't think of themselves as actual criminals.

Imagine if one of these hackers tried to sell government secrets: it's a risky strategy to knock on the door of "Enemies of the State." Chances are, by the time a United States teen hacker exited the Chinese Embassy, someone from the US government would be waiting to ask a few questions. Not a great way to keep a low profile. And these guys did want to preserve their anonymity; they knew how quickly Federal agents could shut them down if they caught you. The penalties for hacking weren't very well-defined back then but every fifth grader knows that "treason" – even in America – is an off-with-your-head sort of offense.

Speaking of law enforcement, it hadn't quite caught up with hacking yet. It's true that in 1984 the federal government first criminalized certain computer crimes, but between 1991 and 1997 only about 200 cases were investigated. The questions which were still being asked back then were:

- What should the penalties be?

- What kind of damage is possible?

- Is there a way to legitimately claim damage with no financial loss involved?

Behind all these questions was another:
- How much *could* hacking really hurt anyone?

Of course, companies and individuals were angry about having their networks disrupted by worms like Morris and, later, having their data obliterated by viruses like Melissa. They wanted someone to pay, but there still was no sense of the incredible damage that could be done by a lone hacker tromping with malice through a company's network. The idea that a hacker might put whole companies – and nonprofits – out of business, which now happens many times a year in the United States, was not even realistic at that time.

This Hacker History takes us up to about the year 2000. Unfortunately, since then, things have become much more complex.

ORGANIZED CYBERCRIME

Question: What happens to every kind of commerce over time? Any economist will tell you that as long as there is an ongoing supply and demand for any product, some kind of marketplace will eventually develop. In some rudimentary fashion it will organize itself. And this isn't something a mafia godfather has to plan or even think about. When we say that cybercrime is "organized" we don't necessarily mean that it's been taken over by "Organized Crime," although surely the mafia are involved in some aspects of it.

How does this self-organizing principle work? By example, let's consider the story of an ancestor who has decided to settle down and become a villager. Suppose she was a Eurasian warrior woman who is ready to hang up her saddle. A year later she has an extra horse to sell. Do you suppose she knocked on all the village doors to find the one family who needed an extra horse? It's possible. But somewhere in the same village was someone who wanted to *buy* a new horse. He may have knocked on a lot of doors, too. Eventually though, enough folks with extra horses and chickens and barley showed up and congregated in one place. That corner of town became the village market, and now the buyers and sellers could find one another. Pretty soon all the livestock were on one end and the grain was on the other. Voilà, a nicely organized market.

And so it has also become with cybercrime and cybercriminals. As people learned to illegally extract money from, say, a credit card number, bank account, or business secret - like where Starbucks plans to put their next three stores, or the recipe for Coca-Cola

- the demand for these things grew. Hackers got busier, and the supply increased. The "supply" in this case is any data from which value can be extracted. The word quickly spread: a good Internet scam can net two million dollars in under twenty-four hours.[1]

Not surprisingly, this is about the time that cybercrime incidents took a gigantic leap upwards. In fact, a "Cybercrime Calendar" would look something like this:

- 2000 to 2005 – Slow steady increases in the total pieces of uniquely different malware added to the Internet universe every year.

- 2006 – Yikes! A sudden growth spurt up to 200,000 pieces of unique malware in one year.

- 2007 – Triple yikes! An exponential (10 times) increase up to 2,000,000 pieces of unique malware distributed over the Internet in one year.

- 2011 – Somewhere between 17,000,000 and 180,000,000 million unique pieces (depending on what you consider "unique") of malware were released into the Internet Universe.

Imagine the levels of data-stealing that all this malware enabled. What evolved was a very sophisticated marketplace for stolen information and control of our computers.

THE DEVIL IN THE DETAILS

Here's how it works: Hacker Hal has 50,000 data records to sell. They consist of credit card numbers, names, and phone numbers. His theft has not yet been discovered, so these records are worth top dollar (since the cards haven't been cancelled yet). Based on where he stole them (the country, type of card, etc.) each record is worth $17 on the underground equivalent of eBay.

---

1 And this was true by 2007; in 2011 one credit card scam netted the cybercriminals $14 million in just forty-eight hours.

Hacker Hal sells them to a middle man. This makes sense because Hal has a whole team of hackers, and he likes to keep them busy chasing the next chunk of valuable data. Meanwhile, Middleman Mo takes these records and links them to databases which add addresses to each one. He groups them by neighborhood, ranks them from wealthiest to poorest, and sells them to contacts (usually teams) who will actually use the cards. He has spent considerable time on this, but his efforts have increased the value of each record to between $30 and $65 each, depending upon the particulars. Not a bad profit.

Hal lives in Romania. Do you suppose they care about hackers? Sure they do. The police there wish there was a special hell for hackers, because they keep getting hassled by cranky foreign government officials insisting that they crack down on them. But the government is a little too busy populating its prisons with armed robbery suspects and citizens who spawn civil unrest. There's not much room left for (ho-hum) hackers.[2]

Plus, to be honest, the local cybercriminals are bringing a lot of cash into the economy. So while they shouldn't defraud those poor foreigners, it is not a terribly urgent problem. The conversation at the local police station might go something like this, "Hey Stan, give Hal a call and tell him Interpol is harassing us again! He could at least *try* to fly under the radar a bit more."[3]

LAST STOP IN THE FOOD CHAIN

Finally there are the guys who actually get their hands on the identities, the card numbers, or the cash. Often our identity information – sometimes correlated to our Facebook and other social media pages - is used to break into online bank accounts (especially for those people who use their pets' names or kids' birthdays as passwords!). Also, cybercriminals can purchase access

---

2 To be completely fair – Romanian law enforcement have been trying.
3 Romanian law enforcement have done quite a lot to help other governments, but they are quite
   overwhelmed: www.wired.com/magazine/2011/01/ff_hackerville_hackerville_romania/

to our computers. If someone has successfully installed a Trojan on our PC through an email we opened – which may have been sent to us from a friend's hacked account – our system now is controlled remotely by a botnet. Once the botherder has control of our computer in this way, he will rent it out to the highest bidder.[4]

There's more bad news here: the person who rents the use of our computer doesn't even have to know exactly how it's done. Anyone who's willing to risk imprisonment can dabble in cybercrime these days; they needn't be technically skilled at all.

HELP FOR HACKERS

Hal was lucky: his parents managed to scrape together enough to pay his way to Hacker Camp in his last year of high school. This is a good thing, because Hal hadn't realized the true potential of the Internet before Camp. But he certainly knows a good business model when he sees one.

In fact, Hal didn't exactly graduate with honors. More of a lover than a fighter, Hal will admit after his third drink that he finished dead last in his hacking class. But you'd still be wrong to underestimate the harm he can do.

Comfortably supporting his son Joey and his wife Olga, he has a relaxed work-at-home schedule with three-day weekends. He skips Mondays altogether because his favorite day of the week is Tuesday when Microsoft announces all the security holes in their products.

Hal *loves* Microsoft. And it's not just for the Excel spreadsheet he uses to track his profits. It's the fact that they are so many places at once: they provide a wildly popular operating system, browser, and multiple applications. On so many systems! With so many users! And to pay for Joey's soccer camp and his wife's spa treatments, he really doesn't need to take advantage of more than just a few software vulnerabilities a month.

---

4 This is pronounced "bot herder" as in, a shepherd for bots.

Plus, Microsoft does all the work of figuring out the problems in its own systems (with quite a bit of help from the antivirus companies that are catching malware). We might assume that as soon as Microsoft announces a "security hole," everyone would rush to patch it. But they don't. The majority of people take *over two years* to get around to it. A lot of "Patch Tuesdays" go by over two years, and this makes Hal pretty happy.

So, Hal picks a vulnerability (or two, or three) off of Microsoft's list and goes online to find a hacker who wrote code to exploit it.[5] Some hackers offer their malware for free (usually as an advertisement on how good the hacker's other programs are) or for rent or purchase. Hal buys some. Now, how is he going to distribute it? How does he actually get his infection onto our systems? There are basically three ways:

- **Infecting our PCs, laptops or smartphones via legitimate website** – a legitimate site which he has hacked into and inserted malicious code onto

- **Infecting us via a new website** he has set up himself (or rented) to deliver malware

- **Infecting our devices via email we receive** and enticing us to:
   - open an infected file or

   - go to an infected website and see what our favorite airline or hotel has to say to us (this is "spoofed" email, where it appears to be legitimate but points us towards an infected site)

---

5 A "vulnerability" in this case is a software security flaw which allows a hacker using the correct malware or set of commands to gain high-level access to your computer.

There are other methods, but these cover more than 90% of how most of our computers get infected.[6]

BOTNETS AND TROJANS

Before we delve more deeply into Hal's exceptionally profitable business model, there are two cybercrime concepts we need to understand. The first one is the idea of a Trojan.

A Trojan, just like its namesake the Trojan Horse, is a malicious piece of software that rides in on another piece of software. This other piece of software might be a game or a print driver we need. Like the nifty gift horse the Greeks gave Troy, the print driver looks friendly enough. We download it, and the Trojan rides silently in with it.

Or, very commonly, we don't even know the Trojan is downloading. This technique is called a "drive-by download." It occurs when we visit an infected website. Our computer accepts a virus because it doesn't realize that is what it is doing. Basically, while the computer is distracted doing something else, the Trojan sneaks in through a software security hole. Unless we have really excellent anti-virus software, we won't even know it happened.

The process of infection-by-website begins with the way our computers are expected to "load a web page." In order for a website to show up nicely, the Web server – upon which the Web pages are loaded (in the form of hypertext markup language or html software code) – needs to know what kind of browser we are using. The Web server also wants to know what kind of software is active on our system. Why? Because we love to be entertained with the latest visual graphics and audio files, and web designers know this. They try to use the latest and greatest software available to make their Web pages stand out and grab our attention. But in order for us to view those cool effects, we must have software

---

6   Other tactics come into play for large companies with valuable assets or even small companies with lots of money in the bank, but in general they are too much work to apply to the average user's system.

which interprets the Web page correctly. At any given time there will be at least some people with new software, but a designer can't design pages only for people who have the latest cool stuff: The business paying the designer wants the Web page to load and display nicely for anyone and everyone willing to spend money. This means that if we dial in from a system with old software on it, we will be downloading different files than we will download from a brand new PC or Mac. So every Web server must have multiple versions of the Web page which it is prepared to offer.

Question: How does a Web server figure out which browser and other software we have on our computer?

Answer: It pings our system and asks in computerese: "What software are you using? Which version?" and the Web server uses the answers to decide which files to serve up. All of this happens quickly - in the time it takes a Web page to load.

So while we are browsing the World Wide Web, our computer is expecting to be interrogated. But, here's how that goes with a malicious website (one set up by cybercriminals):

Wanda the Wicked Web server: Which browser are you using?

Carmen the Clueless Computer: (version number)

Wanda: Do you have Adobe Flash Player?

Clueless Carmen: Yes, version ___.

***Wanda:* Look, here's a piece of code you should load.**

Clueless Carmen: Duh…okay. (Carmen's job is to accept any code that she is given…she doesn't realize she has downloaded malware.[7])

Wanda: What's your version of QuickTime?

So our computer dutifully executes the code. The code turns out to be a piece of malware that knows exactly how to sneak through a security hole in Carmen's specific version of Adobe Flash Player. This code is called the exploit, and it carries along with it the Trojan. The Trojan hides until 3:00 a.m., wakes up,

---

7 When your antivirus software tries to warn you away from a website, sometimes it's because it is aware of infected code on the website.

and reaches out to its master – the botherder (the botherder is also called "command and control" by anti-malware companies). Our bad boy botherder – let's call him Boris - gives the Trojan further instructions. Then the Trojan erases its tracks and goes back to sleep until the next night. Boris will probably require the Trojan to take screen shots (a copy of the screen, saved to a file) any time Carmen's owner goes to a banking site and deliver those files (containing passwords) to him. Boris will also ask whether Carmen is part of a network or not. If she is, he will try to get her to introduce him to her sister systems.

Every night the Trojan reports back to Boris with all the information it has gathered the previous twenty-four hours. If there is nothing interesting going on with Carmen (for example, no good banking details to steal) the Trojan can still send out spam full of infected links every night. This earns Boris money. And Carmen has now become his latest zombie – a bot in a million-unit botnet. Botnets are on-line armies for sale: Boris will rent segments of his botnets to other people for the purpose of sending spam once he has extracted everything he wants from the computer.

HAS IT HAPPENED TO YOU?

At the time of this writing an estimated 72 million systems in the world are under the control of cybercriminals, unbeknownst to their owners. Is one of the systems yours? Once this occurs, every keystroke is potentially visible to cybercriminals. Not only that, but everyone you email or electronically touch in any way (via USB plug-ins, mobile devices, shared network, etc.) can be infected.

What are all the negative ways this intrusion might affect you? The answer to this question is not always obvious, and it's scary enough to deserve its own chapter.

CHAPTER 4

Hacker Hal Gets Rich – Turning *Your* Data into *His* Money

FACT BOX: A "sinkhole" is a popular method used by anti-malware companies to determine how many zombies there are in a given botnet. The easiest way to explain how sinkholes work is that the good guys hijack the address used by the botherder for long enough to count how many computers try to say "hello" to their leader. A large botnet might have as many as seven million zombie systems in it. The first large botnet of Macintosh computers was discovered by Kaspersky Lab (and reported in April of 2012) with over 600,000 zombie systems, half of which were in the United States. At that time, the botnet had been in operation for at least two years.[1]

THE WALKING DEAD: WHEN YOUR SYSTEM IS A ZOMBIE

In the last chapter we looked at some basic methods used by cybercriminals to hack their way onto our computers. Whether this happens because:

1.) we've clicked on an infected web page which was
   - set up by cybercriminals or
   - a legitimate website which was hacked by them[2]

---

1 For an excellent paper by Jose Nazario on all the methods used to detect levels of botnet infection,see: http://ddos.arbornetworks.com/2012/05/measuring-botnet-populations/
2 Such as: Target, CNN, Washington Post, TIME, etc. – all of these have been infected at some point.

2.) or, we opened the wrong email – it *looked* like it was really from UPS! (Caveat: It's easy to put logos from any legitimate company on an email – for tips on how to ensure it's legitimate, go to Chapter 9) – or

3.) we plugged in an infected USB

the fact is, as soon as our device (cell phones included) has been compromised, the cybercriminal has won some level of control over our system. The first thing the malware will do is neutralize the antivirus software so that no future anti-virus updates will affect it. From then on, the thieves can count on receiving information regularly from the zombie.

But what does this mean exactly? What do we have to worry about if our computers become zombies (or "bots") in a botnet? Understanding what cybercriminals do with their bots can boost your motivation to protect yourself and everyone else you care about. If you think this is a rare occurrence, in the first half 2012, it is estimated that over two-thirds of every system which was connected to the Internet was attacked.[3] And if you are paying attention so far, you know that the number and frequency of attacks is spiraling upwards, not downwards. So based solely on the probabilities, your internet devices will likely be infected sometime soon, if it hasn't happened yet.

GETTING THEIR HANDS ON THE MONEY

Now we'll explore the last step in the process for cybercriminals: how do they make money from compromising your system? There are several methods to turn access into money:

- They might install software which causes a "scareware" message to pop up like: "your system has been infected! Pay $29.95 to download anti-virus." You pay, they make money.

---

3 Here is a link to the article: http://www.kaspersky.com/about/news/virus/2012/Every_third_computer_in_Western_Europe_and_North_America_attacked_while_online_in_the_first_half_of_2012

- They may rent out the use of your system to other people – most often so that your PC will send email. Their options are:
  - Emails constituting part of an attack to overload someone's Web server (called a Denial of Service attack, because when a Web server becomes overloaded it denies service to new requesters, meaning the website goes offline) OR

  - Emails that go out with a message like "Hey, check this out" to everyone in your address book, or everyone in an address book that is provided by the botherder. These emails will contain infected Web pages so that if opened, they will download malware onto new computers.

- They may comb your system for identity details such as Social Security numbers and banking statements so they can steal and sell your identity.

- They may wait until you open a banking or financial site and then copy the information so they can later break in and transfer money to themselves.

- They will try to jump from your system to any other systems or devices on the same network. This may include installing malware on USBs, CDs or other media.

- They may attempt to clone themselves and jump via email to your contact list.

Cybercriminals can also sell access to your system or the data they have gathered - your bank account details and credit card numbers - to other cybercriminals. But regardless of who does the actual stealing, in the case where they are able to get to your bank accounts, they have to get the money out.

MONEY MULES

The last step of the process is the Money Mule. Someone has to take this job in order for the cybercriminal to succeed. The Internet ad (in the employment section) goes like this: "Click here to make big money working from home!" Often the ad does double duty for cybercriminals: while it entices them to become a Money Mule, it also takes the applicant to an infected website so his or her system becomes a bot (and possibly another identity is stolen).

The idea is simple enough. The company breaks it down like this:

- Open a new bank account

- We transfer you money!

- You keep 10 % or $250 per transfer, whichever is less

- Within the time period we specify (usually 3 hours or less) you transfer the rest to our offshore account

Accepting the job means Susie, the college student, or Marge, the single mom, is now employed and working from home! It's all quite fabulous until the FBI comes knocking on the unsuspecting Mule's door and drags her off to jail for aiding and abetting cybercriminals. It's a crime to assist with a crime, and our government believes that when we're being paid to merely make money transfers – especially to other countries – we ought to suspect something isn't right.

Only a few years ago, Money Mules were asked to transfer money in amounts under $10,000 because those amounts aren't usually flagged by banks. But eventually the Feds began tracking funds of any amount which were transferred to countries like

Romania. So cybercriminals got smarter: they hired Mules to transfer money multiple times between accounts in the United States. The final U.S. account where the money ends up might be managed directly by the cybercriminals, and before sending the money to the Ukraine (which is a red flag to banks and Federal agents), they might put the funds in a bank in Paris or Peru. This still works quite well for the cybercriminals, especially when they are taking as much as $435,000 as they did when they put an entire tool company in Georgia out of business. A few years ago Money Mules were sentenced only to probation, but lately they have been receiving prison sentences.

CHECK THOSE CHARGES!

Another clever way cybercriminals can steal money is by getting credit card numbers and charging them in small, regular amounts that might not be noticed for years. For example, Darlene doesn't look at her credit card statement very often. Her payments are automatic. It took her almost three years to realize there was a regular, non-descript charge for $1.71 per month. Of course she was able to get that stopped, but the bank would only refund the last 60 days of charges. Imagine how much money a cybercriminal can make this way if he is able to get away with it with tens of thousands of cards at a time.

Using Trojans and Money Mules, cybercriminals stole over $100 million in one year from small businesses, city governments, and even a special needs school in the United States.. Hackers placed a priority on accounts with over $5,000. Once the money leaves the country, there's nothing a bank can do to recover it. This put companies, charities, and at least one special-needs school district out of business.

IDENTITY THEFT

Here is a worst case personal scenario: You are about to leave on a trip with friends or family. Everything is set. But when you go to the bank for cash the day before your departure, you discover that you have neither cash nor credit. You will forfeit your pre-paid vacation if you don't go. This is sure to create stress, although if you have savings or credit elsewhere you can at least go on your trip. If you are lucky, when you return you will get most of it back. Fortunately for private citizens the bank assumes some liability, and if you can prove that the lapse in security wasn't your fault the bank will refund your money. At least eventually – in the meantime it may take letters, calls, and possibly the help of a lawyer.

Criminals can also steal money from other people using *your* identity, just as you might be fooled by a gang using the identity of someone else. In August of 2012, the FBI reported:

Lawyers' Identities Being Used for Fake Websites and Solicitations

09/14/12—A recent scam has surfaced in which the identify of a Texas attorney, who had not practiced in years, was used to set up a fake law firm website using the attorney's maiden name, former office address, and portions of her professional biography. Other attorneys have complained about the use of their names and professional information to solicit legal work. All attorneys should be on the alert to this scam. If you become aware of the same or a similar situation involving your name, you should immediately report the incident to local authorities, and the FBI at the Internet Crime Complaint Center. Additionally, be sure to closely monitor your credit report or bank accounts to ensure that your identity is not the only thing being stolen.

HACKING A COMPANY

The question of what hackers have to gain from breaking into businesses will be answered in Chapter 10, but a hacker living in China can sell business ideas and other types of "intellectual property" he or she has stolen (like patents and blueprints) to the Chinese government. It's a nice living over there, because as long as hackers promise to only hack outside of China they'll never get arrested and they will be well paid. It might seem like a great place for unemployed hackers to go also, but chances are there's no shortage of Chinese cyber-thieves. According to the FBI, the Chinese government has been training hackers for over a decade.

MOTIVATION TO AUTOMATE!

Hopefully what you have learned so far motivates you to find ways to be safer. Fortunately there are some very easy rules to follow which can go a long way towards ensuring you won't be infected by bad websites or emails. The rules are summed up in Appendix I, but for now you should know that a top-notch anti-virus can block most malware before it gets onto your device. You can also flip a few switches on critical applications like your operating system, Java, and Adobe Flash Player and they will automatically accept updates which improve your security.

But before moving on to ways to fix security problems through software, let's calculate how large our financial losses might be.

CHAPTER 5

Everything We Have to
Lose – Estimating Our Exposure

> **FACT BOX:** Every year, cybercrime exerts a silent but profoundly negative effect on the U.S. economy. On average, each successful intrusion now costs companies between $5 million and $8 million per data breach, and those are costs which flow down to the consumer. But the U.S. government is also losing billions to cybercriminals every year. In 2010 the IRS paid **$5.2 billion** in fraudulent tax returns. In August of 2012, the inspector general estimated that based on past behavior and deficiencies in detection, the IRS would likely pay out an additional **$21 billion** in fraudulent tax refunds over the next five years.[1]

Now it's time to get practical! We've taken a good long look at the Internet-infused world we currently live in and by now you understand how persistent cybercriminals can be. The next big question is important because it's not obvious. If a bad guy has successfully infected our computer, our kid's computer, our home network, or the computer of someone who has our information - what does that mean? *What do we have to lose?* Believe it or not, we can actually quantify this to some extent.[1]

---

1 http://www.cnbc.com/id/48462508/Tax_Scam_IRS_Pays_Out_Billions_in_Fraudulent_Refunds

FINANCIAL LOSS

We've discussed what it means to get infected, but so far we haven't explored exactly how badly that could hurt. To determine the personal financial impact, here's what we need to consider:

- How many credit cards does each household member have?

- What's the total credit limit if they are all added up?

- What is the total balance of all accounts that are accessed online, including 401K, IRA, brokerage, savings, college savings, checking, etc.?

Now let's do a tiny bit of math to figure out what an average person's risk might be.

The average consumer in the United States – let's call her Meredith – has four credit cards. For the purpose of this exercise, let's say that each card has a $5K limit (one recent study puts the average credit card debt per U.S. household at $15,000). Meredith also has $50,000 in retirement, and $4,000 in checking, savings, and investments. If we add all these numbers together they equal the actual cash amount that a cybercriminal can steal from her. Using our average numbers we get a total of $74,000.00.

Next add the $6,000 it will cost her in fees to fix what the cybercriminals do to her accounts (this will involve having a lawyer write some letters). Finally, let's add in the value of 100 hours of Meredith's time filing police reports, writing emails, and making calls. According to most experts, 100 hours is a low estimate of the amount of time it takes to reverse the problems of a stolen identity. Meredith's time is worth $20 an hour, so add another $2,000.

Now we are up to $82,000, plus a whole lot of aggravation. This is average risk per person. If there are two adults in the household, the potential loss just doubled to $164,000. This is what we stand to lose if a cybercriminal is able to crack into all of our accounts and we aren't successful at defending ourselves.[2]

Masquerading as another person – by using credentials such as Social Security numbers or passwords – in order to steal money is called "identity theft." This is the most common way for cybercriminals to steal from us. Here are some typical scenarios:

1.) A person with our computer log-in information logs into our credit card or our checking or investment accounts and is able to steal our money (by transferring it to his or her Money Mule, the usual scenario)

2.) A person with enough detail about our lives is able to *guess* our passwords and break into our accounts as if he or she were us.

3.) A person who has our details opens **new** accounts and begins charging items which we will be financially responsible for (unless we can prove the charges aren't ours). As the first proof of our innocence, we are usually required to file a police report.

4.) A person invents a new online persona using photos of us or personal details about our lives as the basis. This is usually done as a way to victimize others for various reasons. This would be upsetting to discover – especially if it involves photos of our children – but it may or may not have any financial consequences.

IDENTITY THEFT AND HOW IT HAPPENS[3]

Now we know what we have to lose and what the cybercriminal is most likely to do with our data if he or she can get it. There

---

2 By now you can probably see why it's a good reason to use different passwords for some accounts than others. Skip to the Password Protection Section of Chapter 9 if you are ready to act on this today.

3 Just to be clear: stealing someone's identity is one popular method cybercriminals use to steal money. As previously discussed, cybercriminals can also crack into our bank accounts if they have succeeded in installing malware on our computer which records our keystrokes.

are two more questions which need to be answered in order to estimate our risk:

- What are all the ways in which they can get our information?

- How likely are they to succeed?

In other words, what is the overall probability that we will be victimized?

This is a tough question to answer accurately, even for businesses. But it's still a great question to ask ourselves because it should get our families, households, small businesses and charity organizations thinking about all the things we do every day which add to our risk. Even small changes we make in our behavior can have a big impact on improved cybersecurity. When people realize what's at stake, they often become highly motivated to help themselves and their village.

GETTING OUR DETAILS

When it comes to data theft, there are four basic methods today which have been successful. Hacker Hal or his brethren, Feng from China are busy in these ways:

1.) He takes our data *directly* from us. He infects our computer (or cell phone) and finds our personal identification information. This could be from files we have saved or by having his Trojan record our keystrokes.

2.) He finds our data online. Betsy has 17 photos of her dog Sadie on Facebook. Guess whose name she uses as a password on all her accounts?

3.) We give our identity details directly to him. Believe it or not, lots of people are willing to disclose their Social Security numbers when they think they have received an email or phone call from their state lottery personnel or tax assessor.

4.) He steals our data from our own employer – whether we work full time, part time, or pro bono, our details exist in the company's human resource records. Companies of all sizes in every geography are constantly under threat from guys like Hal and Feng. These guys will break in to see what they can pilfer, and employee IDs are just part of their fun.

5.) He steals our numbers from Butterballs: Hal and Feng are also constantly attempting to break into repositories of credit card numbers or Social Security numbers held by major department stores, hospitals, insurance companies, etc.

Let's consider each of these, in turn, and what we can do about them.

We've already discussed the first example in Chapter 3: how Hal and Feng can infect us directly. We will deal with the second and third scenario (primarily when teens post too much information on Facebook, and the elderly are scammed over the phone and email) in more depth when we discuss cyber-predators in the next chapter. Method number four, when our employer is hacked, is covered in Chapter 10 "On the Job." In this chapter, we'll focus on Method number 5, where our personal data is stolen from companies we trust to protect it. This one is unfortunately common for a number of reasons, but there are fortunately some steps we can take to soften the blow when it happens.

HACKABLE BUTTERBALLS

What are the chances our data will be stolen from a Butterball? To answer this question there are two probabilities which should be multiplied together, and the first part we can't do anything about. That is, what are the chances that a company that collects and holds personal identification information will be hacked?

Companies everywhere are under attack as cybercriminals, especially those from China, try to breach their security and steal company secrets, identities, and everything else they can get their hands on. According to an article by Bloomberg in 2012, despite spending over $60 billion on defense systems, there's no end in sight. Companies of all sizes are regularly being breached. Undoubtedly one with your data will be breached, too, it's only a matter of time. This is a fact we simply must accept.

But there is a second probability where we can exercise quite a bit of control: *to some extent* we can decide *how many* companies keep or have detailed information about us, and we can also decide *how much* information they have.[4] This part of the equation is best stated this way: How many companies have enough information about us that if a thief were to steal it, he or she could access our accounts?

OUR LIVES ON THE INTERNET

Consider all the online activity in the life of Suzanne, a single mother of two. Her son is 10 and her daughter is 14 years old. Suzanne and her daughter both use Facebook. Additionally, Suzanne accesses both personal and work email accounts from home and she checks the school websites for the children's homework daily.

And in any given week she might:
- receive the results of her annual physical exam online
- log into her credit card accounts to make payments
- make her car payment or pay insurance bills
- check her bank account
- look at her retirement accounts
- view her paycheck online

---

4 Unfortunately there are many agencies that insist upon keeping detailed personal information about us, including our government, insurance companies, medical companies, and our employers.

- make all her work and personal travel arrangements online

Suzanne also purchases:
- About one-third of her clothing online
- fifty percent of her children's clothing online
- virtually all their holiday and birthday gifts online

And both of Suzanne's children:
- use email and texting daily
- play online games interactively
- use search engines for school research
- watch You Tube videos
- visit links their friends send to them

Based on this analysis, there are at least seven sites with enough of Suzanne's personal details to result in identity theft if they were stolen (a hospital, two banks, her employer, a travel agency, her retirement fund company, and an insurance company). Suzanne also regularly purchases from at least eight different online stores per year. If all three household members are on the same wireless network, and one of the systems becomes infected, the chance the infection will spread to everyone else is quite high.

HOW BIG IS YOUR INTERNET BOOT PRINT?

Suzanne doesn't want to change her use of the Internet. She considers most of these tasks to be necessities. Even when they are not critical, they make her life easier, more convenient, and more fun. But she is ready to consider "reasonable safety precautions." It will help her and her family decide which rules matter most if they start by asking, for example, what steps would we need to take to reduce the size of our Internet boot print?

Your Internet boot print is everything you have left behind after logging off for the day. Just like a boot track in the snow, there are two dimensions to your personal or household footstep – width and depth. By example, the gargantuan slug from *Star Wars*, Jabba the Hut, proudly leaves a large part of his slimy self behind as he moves around in the world. Jiminy Cricket, on the other hand, can barely be tracked as he hops lightly about. When it comes to the Internet, aim for more Jiminy and less Jabba.

Here are the questions to ask yourself:

- How many different organizations have your data? *This is the width of your Internet boot print.*

- How much data do they have and what type of data is it? *This is the depth of your Internet boot print.*

For example, if a merchant only has a unique user name (one we haven't used elsewhere) and he or she knows we like leopard print boots with a three- inch heel, that's not very harmful.[5] If the merchant has our Social Security number, birth date and address, that's what we could consider a different "depth" of data, and something to be concerned about.

Ask family members to consider these questions for any given day or week: What new companies now have our identity details? What new websites now have a password we use for other important sites? Every time we give companies this kind of information, we have just expanded our Internet boot print. Any time we provide someone with details which can be used to identify us uniquely on the Internet, we have increased our risk. Fortunately, it's not impossible to re-size an out-of-control boot print! Here are some tips on doing just that. Implementing even one of these rules will help.

Rules for re-sizing our Internet Boot Print:

1.) Limit the number of cards used by the family for internet purchases.

---

5 Although you may receive spam promising you an amazing deal on such boots if you will only "click here." This kind of ruse would send you to a site which tries to infect your computer.

2.) Don't volunteer additional data; provide *only* what is absolutely necessary

3.) Give fewer details to the companies we *must* give data to – for example: check the box which states, "Don't keep my credit card information on file" when checking out.

4.) Take back your information from companies: request that companies you have previously purchased from delete your credit card information. Note: depending upon the business, often this is not easily accomplished. In that case, move to the next step.

5.) Cancel cards which have been shared too widely and get new cards issued with new numbers.

6.) Instead of credit cards, use the department store cards of the places you shop (if a department store is breached they will get our numbers anyway, whether the card is in use or not).

7.) Use disposable (pre-paid) credit cards for any online purchases teens must make (bogus sites are often offered to gamers; these can be legitimate, infected, or semi-legitimate, where they charge monthly "subscription fees" after the purchase)

And don't forget four **rules about using passwords** while dealing with these websites, repeated here because they are so important:

8.) Use passphrases instead of passwords. Or at least use harder passwords. See Appendix B for help with this.

9.) Employ three different levels of passphrases while using or cruising the web:
   a. one for inconsequential sites (only because they require one);

b. another one for sites which have any information about you and

c. the third one to use on all the most secure banking and financial sites.

Write all passwords down (cryptically) and store in a safe but convenient place!

10.) Create three different sets of security answers to security questions which match each passphrase. Write all these questions and answers down too. (For example, if you use MyLazyCatBlue, you might be a widow who was born in Madagascar. Your first pet was a crocodile named Oscar, and your first job was as a liaison at the Royal Palace in Monaco (your alter ego may as well have some fun!).)

11.) Never, ever create passwords that come from information which is publically available about you. None of your children's names, birthdays or your pets' names should be allowed. This is especially important to relay to kids. Children and teens are often awestruck at how easily their "secret" passwords are guessed.

If we can make at least some of these changes, we'll experience an immediate uptick in Internet safety. Let's not stop there, however; there are two other areas of possible vulnerability which most of us have control over. They are:

- **How safe is your home network?** Does the wireless router require a password? Do you allow anyone who visits to use it? (Ideally you will check to see that your guests and friends have anti-virus installed and working first.)

- **How well-protected is the data you have on mobile devices such as cell phones and laptops?** Anything portable should have a tough password to get into it and should have a security application with a "remote wipe" feature. This means that if it is stolen, you can ensure that as soon as the thief turns it on the data is wiped out. Of course you will want this to be working in tandem with a backup feature so you can restore the data to your replacement device. Note: this should be enabled upon *any devices which are used by anyone in your household anywhere that person goes.*

- Speaking of which – when household members are away from the home router, **do they use unsecured wireless networks?** If so, make sure they understand that is not the time to do any online banking or make purchases. Even if the network is secured, if it is open to a large number of users – such as at a coffee shop or conference – it should be considered unsecured.

In Chapters 8 and 9 we will discuss more specifically the home environment and how to coax others into making changes that will benefit all of us. Up to this point we've explored primarily the financial ramifications of data loss. Next let's see what we can do to avoid something even worse: the damage done every day by cyber-predators, for whom the Internet is one huge playground.

CHAPTER 6

Why We're So Easy to Fool – and What to Do about It

FACT BOX: The FBI has been issuing alerts since 2007 about online dating scams. In 2012, it reported that these scams were bilking U.S. citizens out of an estimated $50 million per year. The average amount each victim lost was between $15,000 and $25,000. According to the FBI, the targets are overwhelmingly female. However, the large number of websites with advice for men on how to avoid ruses like "Russian bride scams" suggests that men may simply be less likely than women to report their losses.

Ever since the world's first con was perpetuated, law enforcement has acknowledged that "a feeling of embarrassment" often keeps victims from admitting what happened. Sometimes this is because the con couldn't have happened without the victim being greedy, and no one really wants to admit to that. But when it's merely a matter of someone who has behaved naïvely, there's little reason for shame.[1] After all, the concept of trust wasn't such an issue in the smallish tribes that human beings evolved from. We had less to worry about back then because:

---

1 Many people disbelieved the story of T'eo, the linebacker for Notre Dame who said he was duped into believing a "woman" he met online and for whom he cared had died of leukemia in the fall of 2012. But being fooled by online dating scammers happens regularly to older people every day all around the world – so why not to a naïve 22-year-old kid? It took courage on his part to admit publically he was victimized. I hope by telling the truth about what happened he helps others avoid being victimized.

a.) People's reputations were established by their behavior, and **reputations** were widely known and discussed

b.) We grew up with extended family around to **help evaluate others and protect us**

c.) All our dealings were face-to-face, **in person**

Of course all of these helpful tools were pre-technology. Can they be adapted to help us in the online universe? The answer is: "to some extent". Before we go into details on how, let's take a look at why face-to-face meetings are so important.

THE ONLINE HANDICAP

Some good research was done in 2012 which helps us better understand the mechanics of "trust" among human beings. The key question was this: What is the basis upon which we determine whether or not a person we are interacting with is trustworthy, and how much is that affected by whether we meet them in person or online?

A study conducted by MIT Media Lab's Cynthia Breazeal and Cornell's Robert Frank and David Pizarro in September of 2012 provided some interesting answers.[2] First, a game was set up in which people had the option of cheating. A game partner could either be a supportive team mate – and they would both potentially win more – or be an opponent. Before they played the game, the two players met each other. Some of them met in person and others met online. What researchers wanted to know was how accurately players could predict the trustworthiness of their partners.

The net result of the study was that players who met in person were far better at predicting the trustworthiness of partners than

---

2 The study was reported in The Well Column of the *New York Times* on Sept 10, 2012 by Tara Parker-Pope and also in *Science Daily* on Sept 11, 2012.

the ones who only met online. This suggested to researchers that the players' assessment was based upon visual cues.

Researchers filmed the meetings and so were able to categorize the body language of players who later tried to cheat their team mate. A pattern emerged.[3] They then took a robot named Nexi with a pleasant face whom the players met the same way they met human players. One group met Nexi when she was programmed to use the untrustworthy body language. Another group met Nexi while she was only using "normal" body gestures. The result was that regardless of the illogic of trusting or distrusting a machine, when Nexi copied the "body language of distrust", students reported distrust for her. Without that, Nexi was trusted. Meanwhile, the students who met on line were unsuccessful in determining trustworthiness with any degree of accuracy.

This indicates that we do have some hardwired ability to *visually* detect a person's intentions towards us. If we are able to interact with them we are much more able to assess whether they will try to cheat us or not. What the study also proved is that there's no special "uber-instinct" that kicks in to help overcome the lack of visual cues, Without meeting in person, students were simply unable to ascertain (through voice cues or email, for example) whether another player was trustworthy or not. Our biology has not adapted or evolved fast enough to help us form good judgment on the basis of online or voice-only interactions. Knowing this should help us all become more cautious.

Clearly we would all be better off if we adhered to one simple rule:

Distrust everyone you meet online until you have met them. If you do set up a meeting, have it in a public place with a friend beside you.

---

3 If you are curious, here's what they learned: When a person does all of these things in combination, they are likely to be untrustworthy. They lean away and cross arms in a blocking fashion; touching, rubbing, or grasping hands together. They also touch themselves on the face, abdomen, or elsewhere.

It would be great if we could convince everyone who is vulnerable that there is simply no reason to *ever* give money or provide identification credentials to anyone they haven't met. Although this rule wouldn't end all online con games, it would certainly reduce the pool of victims.

A 67-year- old widower in New York was approached on an online dating site by a beautiful young woman. The retired cop, perhaps, should have known better. But he was lonely, and her emails and phone calls were convincing. By the time he realized he was being scammed, he had sent "her" over $50 thousand. After he committed suicide, his son discovered the emails and pieced the story together. With the help of an investigative TV crew, he was able to confirm that the perpetrators were from Ghana. He even found the woman (living in Florida) whose photos had been clipped off the web and "re-purposed" to cheat his father. The son, devastated, said that his father took his own life out of shame. If only his father had known how many people fall for the same scam – the FBI noted online dating scams netted over $50 million from Americans in the period June 2011 through June 2012, and that only counts the cases which were reported.

GENDER AND AGE DIFFERENCES – AND WEAKNESSES

We all have personal weaknesses based upon our life experience, our age, and our gender. To make some gross generalizations, some of the most successful online cons attempt to exploit these stereotypes:

- Men are more easily manipulated by the visual, which is to say that stunning photos go a long way to make them wax romantic (and lose their footing in terms of judgment).

- Women are more easily manipulated by words. There's a reason slick men are called "silver- tongued devils." Romance, frequent communication, and a strong feigned interest can go a long way towards entrancing a lonely widow.

- Children can bond powerfully over fun shared experiences (such as online gaming). They are also susceptible to flattery from people they admire and can be swayed by gifts. **There are lots of ways to give gifts online**, like special powers or gaming credits, which parents may never know about.

- Children are more easily frightened by threats which would seem implausible to adults. The FBI issued a Cyber Alert[4] to parents in February of 2012 warning them about "sextortion." One scam ran over seven years. The perpetrators would threaten to hurt a family's members if the girls did not send explicit photos of themselves; once the hackers received the photos, they threatened to post them publicly if the girls didn't send more. It took the FBI two years to catch and jail two perpetrators of this scam which affected at least 3,800 girls. They warned parents that copy-cat predators are still operating.

Informing others about cons such as these can help more children from being victimized.

POLLYANNA MEETS CINDERELLA AND THE PLAYBOY BUNNIES

Pollyanna[5] was a wildly popular story from 1913 (later a movie by Disney) about an orphan who always focused on the best possible aspects of everything around her. So in her mind, she lived in a world where everything was ideal and beautiful. The

---

4 www.fbi.gov is a great resource to check for the latest scams.
5 Pollyanna is a best-selling novel from 1913 by Eleanor H. Porter about an orphan who practiced the first ever documented "power of positive thinking" via "The Glad Game." The idea was to always find something positive about every situation and to focus on that. It is sometimes also used to describe a person who is naively optimistic.

human tendency to wish for such a life is called "hope" and it's quite normal. But our tendency to bet on it is something we need to watch out for.

There are two specific areas in which Pollyanna-ish thinking can endanger us in the Internet universe. The first one is in the area of romance. This is best characterized as extreme wishful thinking.

Examples are:

- Cinderella's Happily Ever After – a wealthy, charming prince who eschews his wealthy, charming peers and instead marries a poor, uneducated girl. But she's nice so they live happily ever after.

- A kind, generous, naïve Playboy Bunny suddenly only has eyes for an average, out of shape, nice guy.

- A much younger man or woman is interested in your wealthy elderly relative.

WE'VE ALL BEEN THERE

Of course many people have yearned at least once in life to be "rescued". The key is to know when we – or those we love – are going through challenging times and be especially vigilant about NOT letting go of basic online security precautions. We all know that stress and emotional difficulty can put us off balance and make us vulnerable. Being aware of this, we can take measures to add additional protections. Like ensuring that Dad's money is secured in a trust, before he starts online dating or deciding in advance whose advice we will seek if we are going to lend money to anyone. In particular, any person who has recently entered our lives online.

IMPROVISING TRUST SOLUTIONS

Now back to the question we asked at the beginning of the chapter:

Are there ways to adapt our old methods of establishing trust to an online world?

Thousands of years ago, we checked reputations, got help from friends and family, and of course met face-to-face. Here are three rules for adapting those techniques to the Internet universe.

1.) **Webcam, Webcam, Webcam.** These days no one has an excuse for not having a webcam or being able to get to one. For the last several years, every new laptop and mobile phone has some kind of camera embedded. They are also available on the PCs at most libraries, and there are Internet cafes with Web cameras even in third world countries. Worst case, pay a Radio Shack for one in Loser Lover's city, and have him or her go pick it up! Con artists such as the guys from Ghana pretending to be super models should give up at this point.

Using a Webcam isn't perfect because it's a flat image, but it will still help to:

- Ensure the person is of the gender and approximate age he or she claims

- Get a better sense of who the individual is by watching his or her body language

- Allow other people you trust to get a good look - you can record Webcam sessions and email the file to a friend, or have a Webcam session which includes multiple participants

- Validate other details of the person's life – if it's attached to a portable device, it can be taken anywhere to show where he or she lives, the view, his or her family members, etc.

Of course, if it's a really sophisticated scam where someone is specifically being targeted for a large amount of money, an attractive sociopath can fake his or her way through the Webcam test. In that case, insist upon the following additional two protections.

2.) Reputation – close the six degrees of separation

It is becoming ever more difficult for people to hide who they are on the Web. Most of us have some kind of professional persona – there are organizations to which we belong (professional or hobby-related) or there are online profiles or biographies about us at sites like LinkedIn, which anyone can view.

One nice thing about LinkedIn is that it's rather easy to close the separation gap because they tell us exactly who we know who knows someone, who knows the person we are interested in meeting. And we can request that our friend introduce us to their friends, who introduce us to their friends. In this way, by example, a LinkedIn profile with 498 professional connections easily expands to allow us to meet over 7.5 million people! This makes it possible to eventually get to just about anyone. That is, provided that they actually exist.

Public records increasingly are put online by the government (state, local and federal) for ease of access. This includes such things as building permits, property ownership, judgments, and more. In addition, if someone claims to be a contractor or have any other sort of professional licensing (real estate broker, CPA, lawyer, or physician) you will be able to check that online with the appropriate state agency or professional group in the state in which they supposedly operate.

Schools from elementary through graduate school regularly post records of their graduates, and even those that don't often will accept calls for the validation of attendance and course work. They also may or may not have yearbook photos online.

If someone has a decent job and has been working for at least a decade or two, you should be able to find his or her name somewhere on the Web. You should also be able to call the individual's employer to confirm employment.

3.) Meeting our fantasy lover – at least by Proxy

In order to ensure your online sleuthing really worked, you do need to conclude with some kind of direct contact. This will help quite a bit in the case where the person shows up all right on camera, *and* there seem to be online records supporting his or her personal story and identity. This is because in more elaborate scams, the perpetrator will claim to be a person who really does exist.

The solution at this point – if, for example, the romance your mom is having seems to be escalating, it's time for you to meet her new romantic partner.

Of course, the scammer will resist. There will be all kinds of excuses. Perhaps the he is in a different country. But no matter where he is, if the stakes are high enough, you can still get the details of his location and hire a professional to confirm this. The professional could be a private investigator (let's call him Sherlock), a delivery person, a recent law school graduate, or someone you hire to meet the possible perpetrator on your behalf. Sherlock might then accompany the suspect to a bank, police station, notary, embassy, or lawyer's office where a secondary validation occurs. Acting as your representative or "proxy," your representative can photograph the requestor, record that person, assess him, and at the very least, obtain a location. If only the retired cop had done this before wiring tens of thousands of dollars out of the country!

Speaking of hiring a proxy – this is an excellent way to deal with a situation where your child, parent, or friend is caught up in the romance of it all and resisting your help. It should be harder for them to disagree that a professional, objective third party *not* be permitted to make an assessment of the situation when money and physical safety are involved. Likewise, if you realize yourself that you are involved too deeply in a situation to be objective, hire someone to lend a hand and impartially evaluate the situation.

Here is a good list to share with online daters. Major red flags:

1. Anyone asking for money whom you haven't yet met (even if you are sure you are in love)

2. Anyone who has come into your life in the previous two years who asks for money

3. Anyone who suggests you should trust him or her based solely upon what he or she has provided you over the Internet

4. A person who gets upset if you ask for proof of his or her claims, or comes up with stories you are ashamed to repeat to a best friend (i.e., they are outlandish)

5. Anyone your child has met online and become enamored of

THE PRETEND PROXY

If you are able to convince your elderly relative that he or she should be careful, you can also offer to play the middleman when it comes to money. Claim to be the intermediary. Your communication need not be confrontational. Alison, a woman living in Los Gatos, California, lost her entire retirement of $202,000 to "Mark", a man she met on line and believed she would marry. Here's a sample email that should have gone to her fantasy fiancé:

> *Dear ConCreep,*
> *My name is Karen Glass. As a lawyer and family friend, I am the executor of Alison's trust fund which contains her retirement savings. She has asked me to provide you with some funds from that account. I am happy to do so as long as I can confirm the terms under which the funds will be replaced. It is my fiduciary responsibility to manage this process.*
> *Could you please reiterate the details of the situation you are in and your specific request?*
> *Sincerely,*
> *Karen Glass, Esq.*

Set up a quick email account for this (the cover story would be that "Karen" uses her personal email for work that is done outside of her firm). Scaring scam artists usually makes them run, but do be prepared for a consequence: just as Mark became verbally abusive with Alison when she ran out of money, the con will likely communicate directly with the mark again to convince her the intermediary isn't necessary. In which case, try your best to convince your potential victim to say, "Sorry, if you want the money, my hands are tied."

PROTECTING OUR CHILDREN

Of course fooling a kid is not as difficult as fooling an adult. Children not only have much less experience, they also tend to be more trusting and are often conditioned to be helpful and compliant. Especially if a predator pretends to be just a little bit older. As most parents are aware, kids can be especially inclined to be enthusiastic about a friendship with someone who is older than they are but younger than their parents.

One fact to remember is that there are very few instances in which *real* kids are able to arrange a physical meeting with other kids whom they have met online. The majority of children and teens have neither the money nor the over-powering motivation to *travel* in order to meet someone new. Doing so would typically require involvement from parents on both sides. And while friends often agree to meet up online for gaming sessions, when strangers join them, the probability is very small that those strangers – who can dial in from anywhere in the world – will be local.

This is the number one reason to distrust anyone who has reached out to your child and suggested a meeting of any kind. In such a case, it is highly likely that your child is corresponding with an adult. As the examples in the previous chapter demonstrate, adults frequently cross state lines with the intent of engaging in sexual relationships with teens and pre-teens (arrested-development adults portray these meetings as "romantic"). A more challenging situation is where your child knows or believes the other person to be an adult, but hides that information, fearing your disapproval.

I strongly recommend that all parents audit their kids' texting, email and online gaming sessions. See Appendixes F and G for easy ways to set this up. An excellent message for kids to get in life, and the earlier the better, is this: "everything you do online is visible to someone, somewhere. So behave as if what you do and say online is public, because it so easily can be."[6] There's also nothing wrong with letting your kids know that when it comes to interacting with others online, **there's no presumption of privacy in your household**.

---

6 If only Congressman Weiner had considered this before tweeting explicit photos of himself to an "exotic dancer." It's astonishing that he would believe it would be received in confidence!

Now before we get into exactly what rules to follow, let's talk about some of the basic technology which got us into trouble in the first place.

CHAPTER 7

Back When the Internet Was Safe – and What Went Wrong

FACT BOX: The psychologist Abraham Maslow wrote a landmark paper in 1943 about the cause of motivation in human beings. His philosophy, which has been widely accepted, was that the survival needs of a human being must be met before he or she will seek love, happiness, or self-actualization. Thus came to be called "Maslow's hierarchy" and it is illustrated as pyramid of needs. Only after our basic physical needs for food and water are met will we be motivated to move upwards. After food, water, and shelter the next most critical need humans have is for safety.

We've all heard the phrase, "home is where the heart is." It's been repeated now for almost 2,000 years.[1] Hopefully such sentiments are so deeply rooted that all the technology in the world won't change them. In the ideal scenario, home is a safe haven. It's a place where we slip off our pumps or boots or loafers at the end of the day and relax.

But no matter how great our neighborhood is, or how elaborate our alarm systems are, unless we practice good Internet security, it won't be long before cybercriminals are sneaking in like rats across the power lines at night. In fact they may already be "conversing"

---

1 Attributed to Pliney the Elder (aka, Gaius Plinius Secundas born in 23 AD, died in 79 AD), who died during the eruption of Mount Vesuvius.

with our computing devices if not our family members. This invisible invasion can easily escape our notice. At least, until the house is trashed, the cash and jewels are gone, and our teenage daughter is missing. In addition to the losses, it's a heck of a mess to clean up.

Before we look at all the ways to avoid this fate, it's helpful to understand the technical issues which lie at the heart of the problem. This will explain:

- Why a fundamental lack of security was built into the Internet

- Simple steps to increase your protection

And last but not least:

- Why our government can't help us (much)

INHERENT INSECURITY – AKA, TOO MUCH TRUST

Early developers of the Internet adhered to three principles which contributed to security problems. These are:

- Presumed trust – it was expected that users would behave themselves

- Easy access – if you could get into the computer lab, you could get on the network

- Two-way communication – back and forth "pings" between computers created reliable connections

Let's take a look at each of these solutions-turned-problems separately.

GENESIS

The Internet, as we know it today, actually has too many "fathers" to count. Tim Berners-Lee may have put up the first Web page, but numerous brilliant people came before him, like Bob Kahn and Vint Cerf – scientists working for the U.S. government – who created the original concept and developed the tools to make it possible.[2] And former Vice President Al Gore was critical as well – a senator at the time, he's the guy who passed the bill which funded government development of the World Wide Web.[3] This brought the concept to a point where businesses were finally willing to invest. Gore coined the term "information superhighway" as a way to sell us on funding it, and to help people see what might be possible. Most experts agree that what was accomplished would have been impossible for private business to do as quickly, if ever.

GROOVY LOVE - A TRUSTED NETWORK

But back to the beginning with Bob and Vint: a large chunk of the technology Berners-Lee depended upon was developed by the U.S. government in the form of something called the Advanced Research Projects Agency Network (ARPANET). The University of California Berkeley and Massachusetts Institute of Technology (MIT) were two of the early universities hooked into it. At MIT, a posting in the computer lab stated:

"It is considered illegal to use the ARPANet for anything which is not in direct support of Government business ... personal messages to other ARPANet subscribers (for example, to arrange a get-together or check and say a friendly hello) are generally not considered harmful ... Sending electronic mail over the ARPANet for commercial profit or political purposes is both anti-social and illegal. By sending such messages, you can offend many people, and it is possible to get MIT in serious trouble with the Government agencies which manage the ARPANet."

---

2 Tim invented hypertext markup language (html), and created both the first Web browser and the first Web server. Because he used "open standards" – essentially technical "rules" of conduct which no one had to pay for, they were widely adopted.

3 Gore introduced the Gore Bill of 1991 giving $600M in funding to expand the ARPANET. Among other things, a university team funded by t this bill created the first widely used Web browser.

In other words, courteous and ethical behavior was expected of the people who had access to the ARPANET. This seems reasonable in retrospect, since only a (relatively) small number of people were involved, all of whom were government employees or scholars.

LETTING IN THE RIFF-RAFF

However, both the problem and the promise of the Internet is the fact that there are virtually[4] no barriers to entry, and trustworthiness is presumed. It can be logged onto anonymously and at no cost. A positive use of this accessibility would be providing Internet access to education for girls in Afghanistan. If we could do this, we would "virtualize" education to the point where there will be no physically-located schools for the Taliban to blow up.[5] Also, by sneaking onto the uncensored version of the Internet, Chinese citizens have at least a small chance of finding out how corrupt their leadership really is. In fact most people in high-tech would agree that there are a majority of good reasons to keep the Internet functioning as it does (with easy access)[6].

But by now "the problem" should also be obvious: while we want no barriers to exist for "good" people, we'd really like to exclude the bad guys. However, since we can't tell if someone wants to access the Internet for good or evil, we must allow them all on, if we are going to fulfill the Internet's primary directive of "interconnection for all." Thus the open-access model of the Internet is not going to change; it's a problem which we simply must work around.

---

4 Of course people need some sort of computing device and a way to access the Internet (a network), but this is becoming less and less costly.

5 I am writing this the day after the horribly tragic Connecticut elementary school slaying. How terrible if America has also become a country where its people will turn to virtualized education out of fear.

6 Call me a radical, but I'd support a charity which drops or smuggles millions of devices with Internet connectivity into regions where a lack of awareness and education still makes it possible to repress people by denying them voting rights and education.

THE TECHNICAL NITTY-GRITTY

There is no effective method of communication, whether between two computers or between you and your teen, that doesn't require some back-and-forth pinging to establish a connection. This is the equivalent of, "I have something to say...are you listening?" And the response is often either "yes, go ahead" or it is silence, which we can interpret as "no".

The Internet is a huge maze of interconnected systems. Tons of data flow across it every second. When you are communicating something – sending data outbound – you don't get to talk nonstop. You have to send some bits of information, wait, listen, and send some more. During the transmission process, your data is broken into chunks – called "packets" – and interleaved with other people's data. This allows multiple transmissions to occur simultaneously over the same phone or cable lines, which is very efficient.

GETTING IT RIGHT

Along the way, there are systems which are responsible for accepting, acknowledging, and forwarding these "data packets." They are called routers (since they "route" our data). One of their jobs is to attempt to calculate the fastest route for each packet to get to its intended destination. The question: "Which is the fastest way for this email to reach my sister in Wyoming?" functions exactly like a traffic problem, "Is it easier to use surface streets to get downtown during rush hour or to use the freeway?" Since levels of data traffic are constantly changing, and there can easily be traffic jams or computing accidents, routers make these decisions on the fly. Sometimes they are right about the fastest route and sometimes they are wrong.

The result is that your sister's email server (a central computer which "serves up" email) in Florida might receive data packets out of order. The fifth packet of data may be received before the second packet. This problem is solved by including instructions with each data packet that tell the receiver exactly where it fits in the sequence of data – "this is packet number five out of ten" or "this is packet number two out of ten." The email is thus put back together correctly, and it all makes sense. In the event that a packet is missing, the receiving computer will send a message back to the source computer asking, "where is the third packet?" When the missing packet is received, it will be popped into the sequence. This whole back-and-forth communication takes a lot less time than resending entire messages.

BUT WHO'S *REALLY* TALKING?

All of this works very well. But what if Cruel Carl wants to intercept the conversation? If he does, there are multiple places and ways he can slip quietly into the middle of the data stream. He can then intercept information from both sides. In some cases he will just listen, and in other cases he may make changes to the data before forwarding it to the other side. Meanwhile, the computers on either end assume they are having a private conversation.

To illustrate this idea, let's suppose you are Mary, Queen of Scots. Things aren't going well for you after the murder of your husband Lord Darnley, and you'd like to know if you can find refuge in England with your cousin Queen Elizabeth. But you don't want to ask outright, so you invite her to come to Scotland to discuss it. Your trusty knight Sherman rides off with the letter. Ten days later Sherman comes back with a response letter from the Queen. She's inviting you to visit her instead. By this you presume it will be safe, and you pack up your gilded carriage. Unfortunately, upon arrival you are escorted to prison, where you spend the next 19 years of your life. How did this happen? Unbeknownst to you, Sherman stopped in to see a girlfriend in Southern Scotland. While he was there he ran into David, who claimed to be married to one of the Queen's ladies in waiting. Sherman decided he'd rather spend a week with his gal pal than make the long ride to England. So he asked David to deliver your letter for him. The next week David returned with the Queen's response and Sherman took it back to you at the castle and all seemed well.

But in fact, David was an imposter so the Queen received a *different* message from you than the one you sent. The note she opened said, "May I have refuge in England?" and Queen Elizabeth responded, "If you come, I will be forced to imprison you." But alas, this was not the note you received. Both you and the Queen assumed you were talking to each other, but, in fact, David was in the middle changing the messages.

This describes an Internet attack called the "man in the middle" (MIM). There are many forms of this kind of attack, but the idea is the same: some entity in the middle masquerades as both sides of a conversation. In this way the entity can capture passwords, account numbers, and all kinds of other data that is useful for them and injurious to you.

DATA TRAVAILS

Any time your data is traveling over the Internet in unencrypted form – called "plain text" – it is susceptible to a MIM attack. One excellent way to stave off MIM attacks is the use of encryption. If only Mary and Elizabeth shared a private code that no one else knew! Fortunately in the world of high-tech you need not muck around with codes; there are lots of software programs that will do it automatically for you.

KEEPING SECRETS

As soon as people began conducting financial transactions over the Internet, confidentiality became a concern. One obvious solution was to encrypt information.

Encryption is a big and complicated topic with tons of history behind it. You don't need to know all the hairy details – all you need to know is that the technology in this area is quite good, and you can generally count on any reputable company from which you purchase a security product to know which type to use. Every kind of encryption takes at least a little work to crack, and some of it can take years. Security software products usually follow the rule of thumb which states: "make it much more expensive to crack into this data than the data is actually worth." If you're only protecting a home computer and ordinary email – where the most confidential message involves Aunt Martha's secret recipe for rum cake – you can rely on the professionals.

Nuclear launch codes, on the other hand, are a whole separate category. Military secrets are prizes which whole teams of professional hackers spend years trying to get on behalf of their governments. This is one reason the U.S. government doesn't have a lot of resource left to help us out –it has its hands full fighting hackers and cyber terrorists. Even if they wanted to, no single government can possibly manage the behavior of the billions of people who log onto the Internet every day.

As a private citizen, you don't need the toughest encryption in existence. But you should make use of tools commonly available. To understand these tools and how they work, think of your information as a sealed tube of data which has both an address and a return label on it. It could be made of clear plastic so that anyone can see what's in it, but the data bits inside may be mixed up (encrypted). Alternatively, the tube itself could be made of PVC pipe (the solid white kind our sprinkler systems are made of) so that whether or not the data inside is encrypted, no one can see it. If the data is both encrypted (scrambled) *and* sent in a PVC pipe, this is double protection. If the tube breaks, the data still cannot be read. "Breaking the pipe" is what happens when a MIM attack occurs. This can happen over any unsecured wireless network (for example, the wifi at the airport) if there is a hacker who "sniffs packets."

USING HTTPS

To protect yourself from such an attack, try using "https" when you ask for a website. This allows you to both hide your data and encrypt it. Where the "http" of an Internet address is a clear pipe, the extra "s" stands for secure, so no one can see into it. This extra security won't matter if you are merely browsing the internet, but when making purchases or conducting financial transactions, you should expect it. The option will only exist if the company who owns the website domain has invested in the additional security, and in many cases they will also have a plain "http" site as well. So how do you make sure you are using their more-secure https? It turns out to be very easy.

TIP #1

Just insert the s! Instead of asking for: http://bankofamerica. com , ask for https://bankofamerica.com. If the first version comes up when you search for Bank of America on Google, put your cursor on the link in the browser and insert an s. More and more financial sites offer no alternative – you can only visit them securely. For example try going to: http://fidelity.com. You will be forced instead to https://fidelity.com. You can see that http://google.com exists but so does https://google.com . Many companies are moving this direction (only 12% as of mid-2012 but the pace is increasing). Google automatically switches users to https when the user wants to check gmail. Amazon will switch you as soon as you want to buy. Understanding the value of https is simple and important for all members of your household to understand, especially when they are mobile and using unsecured networks.

This is also the reason you should make sure that strangers cannot use *your* wireless network. Many routers broadcast a signal that reaches the neighbors, and even the neighbors' neighbors. It's not hard to drive around a neighborhood and get the signals for multiple networks. If they don't require a password to get on, anyone can use them. And if the intruder wants to sniff for data while they're there, they can.

ONE MAN'S OPINION

Gordon Snow was formerly the FBI's top cybercrime cop. Here are two tips from an interview *USAA Magazine* had with him about safety at home[7]

TIP #2

Rule: Don't freely allow others to connect to your home wireless. Gordon expects anyone who wants to connect to the home wireless to run a security scan FIRST. In fact, here's a link to a free, safe, security scan (http://www.kaspersky.com/virusscanner)

This might be overkill for most of us, but suppose your teen is hosting a party and there are just too many kids to check their individual systems. In this case, change the router settings so that the only devices allowed to use the wireless network are those whose individual MAC addresses have been entered (this is basically a serial number which is unique to each device). Instructions for doing this can be found here: http://netsecurity.about.com/od/quicktip1/qt/qtwifimacfilter.htm

PRIVATE PARTS

Now that we are finished discussing data movement and how to hide it, let's address privacy. Lack of privacy need not be a concern unless there are people out to get us or to get the people we love. Unfortunately, we can't really know if or when this might happen. So it's useful to understand how both companies and cybercriminals collect details about us and our habits.

---

7 You can find the online article here, https://www.usaa.com/inet/pages/advice-security-6tipscybercop?SearchRanking=1&SearchLinkPhrase=security%20tips%20gordon%20snow

WE KNOW WHERE YOU ARE AND WHAT YOU WANT

Nontechnical people often think of a computer as a handheld game or a typewriter (depending upon your generation). It's a tool you pull out and use to entertain yourself or get something done. You push the right buttons, it does what it's supposed to do, and you close it up when you're finished. In another example, suppose you go window shopping one afternoon. Until you actually walk into the store, you don't have to deal with pushy salespeople and they need not know who you are. Unless you decide to step forward and tell them you like their products, they won't be able to come tap you on the shoulder about buying something the next day.

But in fact, computing devices are much more like the transformers of action movies – devices which are capable of waking up and serving masters other than their owners. And Internet shopping does not work like window shopping. You can't look at anything on the Web without also being seen, at least to some extent. People who shop very much online have noticed that our interests sometimes follow us from website to website; the items we placed in the guest shopping cart yesterday somehow pop up in advertisements today.

Likewise, if you travel very much, you will notice that the advertisements you receive are location-sensitive. When you check the English version of Google from Moscow, you will be bombarded with ads offering employment in the United States. And if you are in Vancouver, you will see deals on flights leaving from Canada. How do advertisers know where we are?[8]

There are two tools that help resellers do this. They are not huge concerns in terms of someone breaking into your system (at the present time, at least), but they *are* privacy concerns, so you should know about them.

---

8 This is assuming you aren't carrying a mobile device which has global positioning enabled. In that case the Web server needn't rely on IP addresses.

MAGIC COOKIES AND INTERNET ADDRESSES

You may have heard of cookies. The term is short for "magic cookies" and the idea is quite simple: you go to a website and start filling in a form or selecting items for your shopping cart. As you progress, your computer keeps asking for new Web pages. The website needs to remember what you did on the previous page, so it hands your computer a data cookie with your details on it. When your computer wants to take another step, it hands this cookie back to the website as a way of identifying you and what you want. The Web server continues to add information to the cookie which is handed back and forth. This gives you a different experience than it gives the next person who logs onto the website.

This is a temporary session cookie – it only lasts as long as one website visit. But most websites also want to keep track of what you did last time you were at their website, and the time before. So they will install a long term cookie on your system, too.[9] You can clear these cookies if you want to, but it will make shopping online less convenient.

As of this writing, cookies are not generally considered much of a security threat. Cookies which are used for online shoppers are encrypted by the website using them. This means that cybercriminals are not likely to discover your bra size even if they get onto your system. Cookies also cannot carry malware onto your system. The majority of people choose to allow them. And cookies are how video games keep track of where players are in a game, so they are practically essential for gamers.

The one security caution is that if an "authentication cookie" is stored on your system, and it is hijacked by a cybercriminal, the criminal can masquerade as you to the website in question. In that case the cookie might automatically fill in your login information. This is a good reason not to "save passwords on this computer" when websites offer you that choice. It is also another reason

---

9 Most cookies have an expiry date, but some of them automatically renew.

banking websites usually provide at least one other authentication step beyond simply your log in.

WHERE ARE YOU?

One method advertisers use to figure out our location is to look at our Internet address. To get online your computer needs to open a connection, or a portal to the Internet. It will do this by requesting what is called an Internet Protocol (IP) address. These are long sequences of numbers uniquely identifying your device. Often the company that provides your home with Internet service has a big inventory of these numbers that they pass out to customers. Sometimes an IP address is assigned permanently – for example, if your router will always be on – and other times it is assigned on the fly based on what numbers are available. However, there will usually be a block of IP addresses your internet service provider uses for Northern California (or even, say, the Piedmont area of Oakland) and another block they will use for other geographies.

When you are "on the move" the same thing happens: any given network will have a set of IP addresses it uses. When you get on the wireless network at Starbucks in the Philadelphia airport, the airport's router assigns you a temporary number. Wherever on the Web you go with your browser, each Web server sees you as a stream of data which originates from that specific address. There are databases which connect IP addresses to physical locations. Figuring out who has what addresses gives advertisers at least a rough idea of where you are logging in from. If they cross reference this to the demographics of your area, they can guess even more about you.

Let's wrap up this discussion of technology by summarizing some key points:

- The moment we link to the Internet, a two-way communication has been established.

- We can't stop people with bad intentions from accessing the Web because it was designed to include people, not exclude them.

- Wherever our data goes there is the potential of leaky pipes.

What all this means is that both the data which is saved on our devices and the data which we are sending back and forth (email, texts, etc.) can be stolen if cyber thieves have the right tools and are committed to getting the job done. However, in most cases we private citizens are not worth their effort. If we turn on the right protections and adhere to a few basic rules, we will defeat the large majority of automated tools cybercriminals use to get to us. For tips on additional rules to follow and how to convince the other members of your household, move to the next chapter.

CHAPTER 8

Home, Sweet Home Part I – Rules We Can Live With

FACT BOX: The tendency of most creatures to resist change is a well-documented evolutionary skill. Repeating successful behaviors which have been time-tested helps us to live longer. Yet change is often desirable: when our current behavior works against our own safety, survival demands that we overcome our resistance. And although reward and punishment have their place, education is one of the most effective tools for changing thoughts, beliefs, and behaviors. Explaining the risks inherent in current behavior and offering new alternatives goes a long way towards motivating change.

If you've somehow managed to get this far in the book and you are still not clear about the significant role you can personally play in fighting cybercrime, let me reassure you. There is great value in boosting security in even one household (or personal set of devices).[1] As we've discussed in previous chapters, at least we can save our own financial assets. But there is also a larger problem: the more mobile computing devices we acquire, the more often our data will move between our home and business networks. We take laptops home, we check work email from personal cell phones, and we use our home wireless to download work applications. This trend is accelerating faster than companies can keep up with, and

---

1 Any and every household, whether it's you and your cat, a roommate, a significant other...

employees are reluctant to agree to the restricted use of their own devices.

What this means is that if cybercriminals can successfully infect enough home networks, every business (and nonprofit) in the country can be ultimately compromised as well. Surely most cybercriminals are beginning to figure this out. This is what makes home defense even more significant.

WHY WOMEN?

As the primary caregivers in a majority of households, women are a critical line of defense for our homes. I've spent some time discussing the reasons for this in my blog, www.cjonsecurity.com, but suffice it to say that the fight hasn't been going very well without the fairer sex. And, as everyone involved in Internet security would have to agree, including the US Department of Homeland Security, now is at least a great time for as many people to get involved as possible.[2]

"TOTAL SECURITY" IS EASY

Let's talk about the threat of being robbed. If you want to keep your house from *ever* being broken into, protection is not that difficult. All you need to do is "secure the perimeter." Here's how:

1.) Dig a moat.

2.) Throw in some alligators.

3.) Put up a fence so the alligators don't eat your guard dog.

4.) Add a Rottweiler or a Doberman to the mix.

5.) Lock all your doors.

6.) Don't ever let anyone in.

---

2 The US Department of Homeland Security has a cybercrime program called "Friends of the Stop Think Connect Campaign". More information can be found here: http://www.dhs.gov/stopthinkconnect

7.)   Don't ever let anyone out.

And voilà, we have "perfect security." As long as you are only protecting an ordinary household, you will never be robbed.

But unless we have way too much in common with the Unabomber, this prescription won't work. There are friends and family we enjoy seeing now and then. We need groceries and pizza, so we'd need to let those people in, too. Most of us also enjoy leaving the house. The fact is: our civilized world has flexible boundaries everywhere we look. We go to work, leave at night, and return again. We're also able to easily fly (or walk or drive) between states and many countries.

"Perimeters" that we can cross are inherently insecure. But they are also essential to our happiness: they allow freedom, love, commerce and innovation – pretty key elements of life, right?

This is exactly why there is no perfect solution in the world of security. When no boundaries can ever be crossed, life is unbearable. So the best we can do is "manage" our risk. We'll never reach a point of not having any.

WHAT'S REASONABLE?

This leads us to the question of designing security that we can all live with. What do we mean by this? At least that:

- The rules *can* be followed – not too difficult to implement

- The rules *will* be followed – so they are not:
  - Too complex
  - Too inconvenient
  - Too restrictive

- There is some incentive or motivation to follow them

And you will need a system for checking whether the rules *are* being followed or not. You will need to monitor how well people comply (in high tech we simply call it "compliance") so you can reward people, motivate them, punish them, or change the rules. Let's start with how we get people to follow rules in the first place.

CORRALLING KIDS, TRAINING PETS

Part of the job of mothering includes the task of shaping our kids' behavior. Even if you haven't been a mother, you've probably done your fair share of this work with siblings, friends, mates, parents, bosses, employees, or pets. Traditional tactics of influencing behaviors include education, acknowledgement, rewards, punishment, and consequence.[3] We adapt these tactics to fit the person, the goal, and the situation.

What we know about shaping good behavior when it comes to Tommy washing the dishes or Suzy leaving out the lawn mower is also true with cybersecurity. If we can teach good Internet safety habits (along with the motivation to follow them) *before* our kids leave home to make their way in the world, they are much more likely to use them once they are out "in the wild."[4]

KEEPING AN EYE ON KIDS – WHAT'S DIFFERENT NOW?

In the bygone era of only one phone line per house, answering it was a privilege parents would bestow upon us at a certain age. When that momentous day arrived, they would teach us the proper etiquette of answering a call. We were required to say something like, "Hello, Cleaver's residence, Beaver speaking."

And remember the "busy" signal? If the line was in use, no one else could call. Voice mail didn't exist, and parents scolded teens who hogged the phone. Although inconvenient, there were a few security benefits to this:

---

3 Women don't generally have the "luxury" of having superior strength over their mates so have evolved more complex ways of behavior management than those of the stronger sex.

4 This is a cybersecurity term which refers to the internet at large so that we often talk about the first time malware was discovered "in the wild". For example, "the first version of this virus was first discovered in the wild in 2007."

- Except for face-to-face communication or snail mail, this was the only avenue of personal communication

- Who was calling was considered public information (a younger brother would yell, "Wally, it's your dopey friend Eddie!")

- The conversation often occurred in a high traffic area of the house – it was rarely private

- So in those days, parents knew *who* was calling their kids, *when*, and more or less what it was about.

Obviously things have changed radically since then. These days children as young as 10 routinely carry cell phones and play games online with strangers. If not before, by the time they start high school they've got email and Facebook accounts. They frequently use Skype and Webcams. This creates situations in which:

- Parents often *don't* know who a child is talking to or when

- Parents know even less about the subject matter of these private conversations

- The amount of detail that is shared can be extreme (photos and emails in addition to voice)

- What is shared can be instantly and permanently publicized

At the same time, while it may be argued that exposure to all of this has helped children mature faster, it's not reasonable to believe that in just a few decades our kids have morphed into the teenage equivalent of Yoda.[5] They need our help whether they know it or not. And we may need to remind them that use of the Internet is

---

5 The wizened (and adorable) green wrinkled *Star Wars* creature-philosopher who knew all.

like driving: it's a privilege, not a right, because someone has to pay for the devices, the connectivity, and the protection.

WHEN EDUCATION IS ALSO MOTIVATION

One way to help them understand their risk better is to share a few age-appropriate stories. Search these up on the Web if you need more than those presented in this book. We all tend to be more interested when we understand that rules are actually in place to help us. The cheerleader who is now being stalked in San Jose, California because she befriended the wrong person online can't take back what she did. But her regret can certainly become another child's learning experience.

THEY'RE DEFINITELY TALKING TO *SOMEONE*

This is not a book about parenting, but behavior management and monitoring will be easier if your children speak to you regularly about what's important in their lives. That said, no household Internet security system should depend upon something as fickle as a child's willingness to talk. Even when a kid will discuss what bothers him, he doesn't always know what's relevant. Children rarely know until it's too late that they are being targeted or when.

HALL MONITOR

Kids are used to being supervised and managed. In school, they have teachers and hall monitors and playground attendants. One of the best early lessons for them to learn is that the Internet universe is no different. *Someone* will always be watching, reading, or listening. As a parent, you should definitely add yourself to this list. Under no circumstances should children under the age of 16 be communicating with strangers without being monitored.

OUT IN THE OPEN

When it comes to security, there are two schools of thought on monitoring people. One line of reasoning is that if we tell them they are being monitored, they will behave better. This is the method being used with signs like, "warning: these premises are under video surveillance." We know there are some benefits to this approach: Thieves believing such messages are more likely to do their thieving elsewhere.

CLOAK AND DAGGER

The other approach is to monitor people *secretly*. The idea here is that thieves will work harder to keep their activities hidden if they know they are under surveillance. People are more comfortable and careless when they don't know they are being watched. So we are more likely to catch them if we don't admit we are watching.

These methods can also be combined, with some activities being openly monitored (for example, by camera surveillance) and others being covertly monitored (for example, by employers using software to watch the online activities of employees). To cover both options, most employers these days inform employees that they have no right to privacy in the workplace.

The latter approach can be a good one to take at home also. If you are the one who is:

- Providing the computing toys

- Paying for the wireless and the Internet connection to make them work

- Facing most of the risk

Then why shouldn't regular monitoring be part of the agreement? This also prepares other household members for the responsible use of computers at college and at work. There is no such thing as anonymous Internet browsing, and even the tools which we think will obfuscate what we do online can be defeated.

Ideally, we will help kids learn not to trust the wrong people while the cost of failure is still "affordable." It's much better for them to fail when you are there to help them, than to fail later when that could mean bankruptcy or personal bodily harm.

Of these options, only you can guess the best approach for the people in your life (including elders we care about) when it comes to safety versus privacy. Here are some questions to guide you:

- Do you believe that they have a right to privacy? If so:
  o With what sort of communication and in what ways?

  o At what age?

However, if you are already in a situation of distrust – whether you distrust the motives or abilities of the people in your orbit – I would urge you to apply monitoring software as soon as possible. Be sure to follow your intuition as well.

TOOLS TO HELP

If you decide in favor of monitoring, there are good products which can give you an immediate understanding of what your kids are up to. They are easily installed, but you can also hire someone to do it for you. [6] These products can:

- Restrict access to certain websites

- Monitor their activities

- Send you copies of messages which are received from or sent to them

- Instantly let you know who is calling or texting them

Recommendations for these kinds of products are made in Appendix G.

---

6 See where to hire help in Appendix G.

Let's summarize three key rules we've discussed so far:

1.) We should all presume that every activity we conduct over the Web, email, or texting is being monitored and could be sent to the wrong person or hacked by a criminal.

2.) Any of these communications could be made public at any time. Not just by the *intended* recipient but also by anyone who sees it later. Or, by a hacker who is listening "in the middle."

3.) In the online world, **trust no one**. (This rule has been covered in previous chapters.)

Now we can move to the next chapter to cover the last seven rules of the Fundamental Ten.

CHAPTER 9

Home, Sweet Home Part II – Rules
We Can't Live Without

FACT BOX: Slime mold is an organism -that operates perfectly capably as a single-celled amoeba. But when food runs out, it will group together with other single-cell slime molds to create a larger organism. In this process some of them die, allowing the remaining cells to survive. Scientists have long been fascinated by this example of "altruistic intelligence" operating in nature. Is it possible that human beings' tendency to follow rules for the "greater good" are vestiges of a similar motivation? Whatever their origin, these are useful motivations to capitalize upon when setting up new rules to follow.

In the previous chapter we covered these three rules about your personal and household safety on the Internet:

1.) Presume every Internet activity might be sent to the wrong person or hacked.

2.) Presume every Internet activity or message might be made public.

3.) In the Internet world, trust no one.

Now let's talk about seven additional safety basics:

4.) Most **personal data** we post is interesting to cybercriminals.

5.) We must **be patient** with the tools that are there to protect us.

6.) **Use different passwords** for each "circle of distrust."

7.) **Swirl the url.**

8.) **Let email get stale.**

9.) **Don't use your debit cards at ATMs unfamiliar to you.**

10.) Follow the **online banking rules** in Appendix A.

The good news about this list is that just about anyone who can use a telephone can also learn how to follow the rules.

PERSONAL DETAILS: MORE INTERESTING THAN YOU KNOW

It may not seem significant that hundreds of your online "friends" know how much you love Monty Python, that you buy all your shoes at Nordstrom's Rack, and that you call your grandma Nunu, but these are exactly the details a cybercriminal can use to make others believe they're hearing from the real you. One very successful scam convinces relatives that they have received an email from a loved one in distress. Usually the story is that a niece or grandchild is stranded in a foreign city and has lost his or her money and passport. The uncle or grandmother must send $700 by Western Union so the youth can fly home. These emails are written to sound just like the person whose Facebook account was hacked, where each plea begins with the youth's usual greeting, like, "Dear Uncle Phish."

We also may not realize that once someone knows *one* unique piece of information about us (such as the town we live in) it can much more easily be linked to additional data about us elsewhere. A single data point is like a snowball hurtling through the sticky snow of cyberspace: it can grow very big very fast. With each new piece of information added, the profile becomes more specific and makes us easier to find.

Here's a real life example: a cheerleader from a high school in San Jose, California befriended the wrong person on Facebook. He knew she was a cheerleader, the town she lived in, and her first name. But San Jose is a town of about half a million people, so what's the problem? Well, it turns out there are only eight high schools there with a total of about 10,000 students, and not more than 200 are varsity cheerleaders at any given time. Once a stalker learned her first name, the total number of possible victims had been narrowed down to three. He could have attended a few games and found her, but tracking her down was even easier than that: other people had posted photos of her and named the school. Thus far, he has only sent her taunting emails and photos, but she's afraid, her family is frustrated, and the police are still trying to find him.

The point is that even with a few bits of data from a Facebook page or a few details divulged about our online gaming, the criminal can fill in enough additional data– by finding our friends, locating clubs we belong to, and checking public records – that we could be in trouble. Help your household members understand this. Ask that they let you know about any postings by friends (with details or photos) that might also create problems. Request changes to be made to these postings and images. People very often are willing to restrict access when they understand that the concern is one of security.

One very important alert about photos, that the FBI addressed in a Cyber Alert to Parents in 2012 revealed that many people do not realize that **photos taken with smart phones include a "geotag" of the exact longitude and latitude of where the photo was taken.**[1] This could be a handy tool when you'd like to remember precisely where you were, but broadcasting exact locations to cyber

---

1 Reading geotags is easy; it only requires that a person download the free software from sourceforget. net/projects/geotag/files

predators is obviously a mistake. A child posting a smart phone photo taken at school, and another one taken in the backyard, has just made himself or herself very easy to find. This is also how the mere mention of a family vacation – as long as there is at least one photo that has been taken at home - can lead to a burglary. Geotags can be turned off fairly easily, depending on the phone you have. Put this on your to-do list immediately! It's also worth reviewing all the photos that you or your family have posted which were taken with smartphones.[2]

Household members also need to realize that they shouldn't post any of these things:

- the timing of trips or vacations (when the house will be empty)

- the town or neighborhood they live in, when emailing or talking to strangers

- details of pets, if their names are used for passwords or security questions

- special hobbies or clubs they belong to

- their full name

- details about other family members (especially gender, age or birthday, as in, "my sister just turned 12 today")

- details about family schedules such as where they will be and when[3]

Children need to understand: **any personal information posted to the Web may be relevant to a cybercriminal.** (For young kids

---

2 For a recent report about how one in five Americans are affected by Cyber Stalking, go to: http://www. staysafeonline.org/about-us/news/cyberstalking-is-a-real-crime-one-in-five-americans-affected-by-unwanted-contact

3 In the fall of 2011, the college-age son of an executive at a cybersecurity company was kidnapped and held for ransom. The kidnappers appear to have used information the young man posted on his social website profile to determine where he was and when they could find him. Thankfully he was successfully rescued.

who play online games, see Appendix D for tips about creating fake personas to play from.)

WHEN AN OHM[4] SHOULD BE AN "OM"

The next rule is to **cultivate patience**. In our increasingly fast-paced world, few of us have an excess of this virtue. But when it comes to computer security, it's important. The primary reason for this is that cybercriminals have become quite experienced at "exhausting" anti-virus (AV) software, so that it gets "too tired" to finish its job.[5] If our AV keeps cracking file after file – often malware is enclosed in a file, which is enclosed in another file, which is enclosed in another file, like Russian nesting dolls – and if our anti-virus software can't find malware, at some point it will either have to give up or label the object "good" or "bad." If the AV defaults to "good" but it is wrong because the file is a cybercriminal masterpiece, you are in trouble because your system will receive the malware and become infected. And of course, the cybercriminal is just as happy if the user herself gets tired of waiting and turns off malware protection.

So cybercriminals love it when we get impatient. Here are some of the things your anti-malware should do for you:

- Check out rotten files that come via email, USB, Skype, or text.

- Check to see if websites have been "black listed" for being infected.

- Check the game files your teen is downloading.

While these files are being scanned or the website is loading, your anti-malware software will often let you know what it is doing

---

4 An ohm is a unit of electrical resistance. It's also a sacred sound used for meditation when it's spelled OM or AUM and drawn out like this: "ooohhhhmmm."

5 "Anti-virus software" is software which protects us against viruses, but actually viruses are only a very specific kind of malware (malicious software). These days, to be accurate we should call it all "Anti-malware". But we use the terms interchangeably because that's the way consumers refer to it.

by saying, "Kaspersky is checking this for safety." This is a good time to get a cup of tea. Because you – the user – can always choose to override these efforts if you are in a hurry. <u>Don't ever do this! And, help everyone else in the house understand why it is important for them not to do it either.</u>

The next-to-last, very important protection that can be easily dismissed by an impatient user is software patching. Software updates are distributed to fix security holes in the software you have on your computer. This is necessary because most software programmers aren't able to figure out all the ways their software can be misused or infected until *after* it has been released. At that point, if it's a popular program, we can count on motivated cybercriminals to find all the security holes.[6] As holes are discovered, programmers write code to fix them. But how do they send these fixes to all the people who own the product? The programmers will rely on the fact that we selected the "automatic updating" box when we installed it. This option exists for many popular applications and even for the Windows operating system. We should all use it![7] One last note on this: sometimes these patches require a system re-start in order to become fully integrated onto your computer or mobile device. Even though it can be annoying to shut everything down, it's important! Remind yourself of how virtuous you are as you patiently allow this.

This brings us to the last critical instance which requires patience, at least in order to do it right: password management.

---

6 The more popular an application is, the more computers it will be on. This means cybercriminals increase their chances of infecting more systems. Also, anti-malware companies like Kaspersky find a lot of software security holes, too. Then we tell the software company, "quick, fix this before more cybercriminals find out about it."

7 For instructions on how to do this, see Appendix F. Most people should turn on "automatic updating" on every Windows system. There is even a choice for "security updates only." Turn this on for every application you trust, especially Adobe and Microsoft products (these are very popular products and cybercriminals prefer popular products). Two other companies who are really poor about providing security updates are Oracle, who owns Java (with over 3 billion installs worldwide, so beloved by criminals). Oracle hasn't yet come up with way to respond quickly to Java security issues. The other company is Apple. Even with the discovery of large botnets of Macintosh computers, they refuse to acknowledge that security is a problem. The best way to handle this is to get a good anti-virus for your Mac.

We're all familiar with the constant demands that websites make upon us to cough up new passwords, user names, and security questions. And most of us accept that we are better off for at least having our banks impose these rules. So then, don't defeat their measures by using the same details everywhere else! If you use the same user name and password for every website you visit, once a cybercriminal has hacked the database of your knitting club, she or he automatically has your online banking credentials too. These can be plugged into an automated program that tries your combination at 4,500 common banking sites until it gets a hit.

Consider the idea of "circles of distrust." The concept is simple: be distrusting of all sites. Presume that at some point they will fail in protecting your data from being hacked. Use different passwords for different types of site, and use the toughest ones for the sites that manage your most valuable stuff, whether that is information or money.

THE CIRCLES OF DISTRUST

Start with three concentric circles. Each circle will contain names of different websites requiring passwords. The largest outside circle will be populated by websites we don't care very much about, which also don't have much information about us. As long as we don't use a password-username combination which will get a cybercriminal to any better websites, we have little to lose if that website database is broken into and that particular combo is stolen. So when signing up for an ezine on Goat Rescue or posting comments at *Celebrity Lies Magazine,* maybe I will call myself paparazzipaula and my password will be WhoLovesChanel? These sites also aren't spending a lot of money on security tools to keep our information safe, so let's make sure it doesn't matter.

The next smaller circle is for sites possessing more information about us – maybe enough to pose some harm to us if they are hacked. These might include your personal email, a professional association, or places you purchase from frequently. Maybe with these sites I'll call myself spendthriftsara and use a password of IllSleepWhenImDead.

The smallest circle in the middle of our chart is for the passwords to sites which we consider the most private. This circle of passwords will only be used for our most sensitive accounts like banks and possibly hospitals. Thus, the user name and password combination will remain your secret. But make a list of all three categories of websites. Then, it shouldn't be too difficult to remember which sites belong to which circles.

Write your passwords down somewhere else. The old rule against this ("don't write them down!") only applies to internal threats, that is, when you are more worried about the people you live or work with than you are about cybercriminals. Of course, if you live with thieves, jot down the passwords anyway but hide them someplace clever like the underside of your lingerie drawer.[8]

Occasionally a problem with the circles of distrust arises for a site that you want to access but the site's password rules won't allow you to place it in the right circle. In other words, it won't accept IllSleepWhenImDead because it has too many characters. Plus the site requires "at least one number and two special characters." We experience one of the most aggravating aspects of security when we attempt to visit a site we are barely interested in only to discover it maintains an over-zealous security policy forcing us to make up a whole new password for this one site. Go ahead and complain to the site manager about this, but as long as we add it to our list we can find it again if we need it.

THE BEST PASSWORDS ARE PASSPHRASES!

Here's a little password quiz, courtesy of USAA magazine in their interview with Gordon Snow:

---

8 Don't forget to also write down the answer to your security questions for each site! Although this is more a matter of convenience than security – resetting them usually requires a call to customer service during operating hours. The problem is that security people haven't yet figured out that there are lots of answers that change over time and there are often multiple answers to even simple questions like "what is the name of your pet?"

Which is a stronger password? This one: *H7%doss!* or *MyLazyDogRex*

Believe it or not, the short one will take a password cracker six hours to crack; the longer one will take 317 years. [9] This is nice because it's easier to remember a passphrase than a complicated password. But unfortunately conventional wisdom has not yet caught up to this, or more sites would allow longer passwords and forget their other requirements (that you use numbers and special characters, for example). And they don't. So you will often be restricted to just eight characters. The only good news here is that it's unlikely that a cybercriminal will expend the effort to crack your password when they don't even know your user name. It's the combination of these two factors that creates a strong defense against random hacking. So don't casually give out your user name either.

IS IT FOR REAL? SWIRL THE UNIFORM RESOURCE LOCATOR (URL)

Say "Swirl the Earl" because it's easier to remember that way. Then explain: every single email, text, Skype, or portable document format (PDF) file which has a website address (ULR) in it that we want to click for any reason should be "swirled." Swirling is easy. All you do is gently move your mouse over the highlighted text. (Don't – REPEAT, *don't* – click it, or your browser will take you there.) What will show up instead of the hyperlinked word – which can be anything – is the actual website URL (it will be by itself in a bubble).

The "URL" (the often-lengthy line which starts with http://) determines exactly which website you end up on. Your goal is to **not** end up at the site of a cybercriminal who is dishing up malware. So don't ever trust what you see written on the page! Check to see *exactly* what your mouse reveals when you hover over the highlighted text.

---

9 Courtesy of an article in the Fall 2012 *USAA* magazine about Gordon Snow, ex-FBI Director of Cybercrime.

For example, I may receive an email suggesting that I "Come to www.yourbank.com and enter your password and win a prize!" But when I pull my mouse over the link what I see are that these innocent-looking blue words are actually linked to this website: www.cybercrimegenius.com. In this case, only because the cybercriminal is an idiot, I know better than to actually click on it. Most cybercriminals are smarter than this. They try not to be completely obvious. What you will see is a long string of names and numbers, but the key is to notice whether it goes to the website of any company you recognize.

Now let's look at a legitimate email so that we know how these look.

Sometimes the link and the URL will be the same. If you click on www.marriott.com, and this link has not been connected to anything else, it will take you to Marriott's home page. But it's much more common for companies to send you emails which say, "click here to make reservations" because usually they want to send you to a special section of their website. For example, here was a legitimate link to a promotion on the Marriott's website: http://www.marriott.com/explore-and-plan/travel.mi?esky.comiar_719&veseg=&veof=EP-T&trkend=1#/san_francisco/morning.

You can see by this example why they hide the URL; it's very long and scary looking. However, notice that even within this ridiculously long string of characters you can find: www.marriott.com/ and this is what you are looking for. This verifies that you are going to the right place. **Don't forget the forward slash because it must be there!** When these characters are contained in a longer string of characters, the piece must have the forward slash to be legitimate unless it ends the string (like www.marriott.com does when it stands on its own).

There, **now you know more than 90% of other people do about checking URL!** Teach everyone in your household who uses email or shops on the Internet how to do this, so they can avoid being scammed. [10] [11]

STALE MAIL

Stale email is healthier. Of course we all want to respond immediately to our friends, family, and employer but if you have any suspicions at all that the email might be from a hacked account (often these have short lines like, "check this out!" and point you to a url) you should wait. Likewise, if you get email from someone you don't know with a tempting offer in it, let this kind of email get "stale" for a few hours or days before you read it. This gives your AV a chance to "catch up" and block any new malware attacks. Anti-malware companies are constantly trying to block new threats for you, but your computer has to download the new protection for them to work. If you wait two hours (or better yet, twenty-four hours) before opening your latest email – and you are sure your antivirus is updated – there's a better chance any threats in your email box will be identified and neutralized.

One other thing you should know is that there are many ways to troll the internet looking for bad websites. This is something the good guys (like Kaspersky, Microsoft and other companies) are doing constantly. [12] They will try to shut down the bad websites when they find them, and they will try to warn unsuspecting people away.

In the same way in which anti-malware first finds a virus and then vaccinates your computer against it, your anti-malware will hand your computer a "black list" of websites it shouldn't go to.

---

10 Note: this is not a completely foolproof test but it will eliminate the large majority of fake links. Also, to be even more safe, you can always forget the link in the email and go directly to the main website of every company you wish to visit (by putting its website link in your browser). If you can't find the promo page you are looking for, call the company and it will help direct you.

11 The scam works like this: you get an email where the link looks like it goes to Southwest Airlines. Instead it directs you to a site which has the airline logos but it's really a cybercriminal site. There they ask you to input personal information so they can "send free passes!". If you fall for it, they can steal your identity. Meanwhile the whole time you are on the site, it is pinging your system to see if it can find a security hole to crawl through and infect your computer.

12 Antimalware companies do this, and sometimes they license additional "information feeds" from other companies to increase the number of bad sites – or good sites which have become temporarily infected – which they know about.

This list is constantly being updated. So if you wait for a few days and then go try to open an email which came from a cybercriminal, chances are the website the email is trying to send you to will no longer exist. Cybercriminals don't want to go to prison, so they are continually moving to new locations and trying to obliterate their tracks when they do. So if your anti-virus doesn't want you to proceed to a particular url –don't go!

ONLY BANK AT BANKS

There's another popular scam involving ATMs. It works by attaching a device to the ATM which records your card number. These are called "card skimmers". The latest ones are wafer thin and can be inserted directly into the card slot. It doesn't interfere with your use of the ATM itself, so you won't be able to tell it's there.

Once the cybercrime team has your card number they need your password. The most common way for them to get this is to have a camera mounted nearby which has a view of the ATM keypad. It will record you entering your PIN. Next your information is uploaded to cybercriminals. This happen wirelessly and immediately so that they can be using your card within ten minutes of your ATM visit. Of course they will keep using it until all the money in the account is gone.

Here are two tips to help you avoid these scams:

1.) ATMs at banks are under much more strict surveillance than the unsupervised ATMs at airports, hotels and some markets. Get your money from ATMs attached to the bank if at all possible.

2.) Wherever you are, cover the key pad! In the old days people used to do this, but once it was understood that the password was useless without the card number people, got lazy. Time to get back to basics!

ONLINE BANKING...RULES!

Online banking is great, right? I love it too: it's always available and very flexible. The only problem is that if you are checking it from a system which is already infected, you are giving cybercriminals keys to your vault.

So the first and most important rule is, never conduct online banking from a public computer. But there are also some simple rules you should follow when doing it from your own (trusted) system. Always do the following:

o   Stop if you have opened any suspicious email in the last 24 hours

o   Update your anti-virus (see instructions in Appendix A)

o   Close all connections to websites and confirm that you have been to no "suspect" sites in the last few hours

o   Confirm that the website you enter your information into has https:// in front of it.

o   Ensure your computer is connected through a secured wireless network.[13]

And on a regular basis:

o   Review all your banking transactions at least every three months – every account and card[14]

---

13 A "secured wireless network" is one requiring a password – preferably a complex one – in order to log onto it. Your wireless network at home should be secured. Any halfway competent IT person (or IT college student) can do this for you (or you can do a Google search for instructions, it's not difficult).

14 This may seem tedious if you don't currently do it but if you keep all your information in one place, a quick on-line scan of all financial activity can be easily accomplished in less than an hour every few months. To prepare for this scanning session, follow the same rules as above for on-line banking to be safe.

- ○ Whenever possible, accept the "extra layers" of security your bank offers, such as a security question for every time you log in

    - ▪ You can ask that your bank call you to request confirmation of actions you don't usually take like making wire transfers. (Many banks are initiating alerts on this kind of activity on their own these days, but make sure.)

Okay, that's it with our top 10 rules! Hopefully it wasn't too painful to learn and you have lots of data to dish up to the rest of your household members. If they can learn all 10 and even follow three they will be many times safer than the average home. If they can follow at least the most critical five, you should have very little to worry about. Now let's talk about staying safe at work.

CHAPTER 10

On-the-Job Lessons and
Liability – Whose Fault Was *That?*

> **FACT BOX:** A study by the Ponemon Institute in 2012 reported that 39% of the information breaches experienced by companies occurred as the result of "human negligence." The same study cited that companies are subjected to approximately 100 attacks per week and the cost per data breach is over $6 million. At the present time negligent employees are merely terminated. In the future, they may also be sued for damages as well.

For most people, what we do for a living – or the volunteer work we do – is a key element of our happiness. And whether it is in the form of a paycheck or the satisfaction of improving people's lives, we get some gratification from what we accomplish along the way. The one thing most people probably don't think about is that any organization we work for can be put out of business by cybercriminals. Although fortunately we *can* have some influence on whether that occurs or not.

This chapter is intended to arm you for two scenarios: one in which you or your mate is an employee – presuming that you'd like to stay employed, uninfected, and out of trouble – and/or the other, in which you may be a manager, a small business owner, or a key contributor to a school or nonprofit. It makes sense to start with the biggest problem common to all of these organizations:

For some crazy reason, banks in the United States are not legally liable for fraudulent transfers or charges made by cybercriminals from non-personal accounts. *This means that the hundreds of millions lost to cybercriminals during 2011 put a huge number of small businesses, city governments, schools and nonprofits in North America out of business.*

Don't forget that cybercriminals have no conscience about from whom they steal. Once they infect a business network, they go after three things: money, personal identification data (customers and employees), and business secrets. There isn't a lot of value in the secrets of small organizations, so the emphasis is on stealing money.[1] Because there is no way to recover lost funds, this is the biggest danger grass-roots charities and small businesses face.

Banks could be doing much more to protect all this money, but their incentive is to maximize profits, so they won't voluntarily take on the expenses of additional security. Not unless the laws are changed. For now, the onus is on us to ask for better protection and see that we get it. If you do own a small business, sit down as soon as possible with banking professionals and discuss what additional security options can be applied to your accounts. But let's talk about what the big companies do wrong first.

STUNNING STUPIDITIES – THE LARGE CORPORATION

Multinational companies aren't immune from going out of business because of cybercrime either. Northern Telecom (or Nortel, headquartered in Canada with origins back to the 1800's) once employed almost 100,000 people worldwide and had revenues

---

1 We've already discussed in previous chapters how money is transferred out of accounts once a network or computer is infected. There is nothing a bank can do once the funds have left the country, and cybercriminals are masters at timing the theft just right to maximize their take and get the funds across the border quickly.

in the billions. In 2009, the company filed for bankruptcy. Back then, when a senior security advisor to the company by the name of Brian Shields told reporters that Chinese hackers were responsible for the demise of Nortel, most of the media were skeptical.

But by February of 2012, he was able to prove his allegations, and numerous people have concurred that Chinese hackers had complete access to Nortel's networks for almost 10 years prior to the bankruptcy. Shields says that Nortel was incredibly irresponsible in handing the problem. Nortel did not even bother to inform companies that purchased portions of its infected business about the problems. He said about the Chinese, "When they can see what your business plans are, that's a huge advantage." [2] Brian says that unfair business practices on Nortel's part – Chinese hackers and the Chinese government – brought down the company. Other experts agree that Huawei, the Chinese telecomm company, now second largest in the world (and by the way, provides infrastructure to support a large part of the Internet), had been copying Nortel equipment for years – right down to the duplication of its manuals. One interesting point about this report is that a majority of the media initially found it to be preposterous.

You can read more about the Chinese threat in Chapter 11, but suffice it to say that any large company operating nationally or globally faces these and other cybercrime threats. This may seem like too large of a problem for any single person to assist with, but don't forget that the biggest problem in cybersecurity is human beings, and how poorly we behave.

The reason an employee of a Fortune 1000 company could have an impact is simply because Internet safety education in most companies is almost nonexistent. Just about anything you can do to make noise about this and to advocate cybercrime training

---

2 If you'd like to read more about the Nortel collapse, see http://www.cbc.ca/news/world/story/2012/02/15/nortel-hacking-shields-as-it-happens.html, http://www.theglobeandmail.com/technology/tech-news/nortel-turned-to-rcmp-about-cyber-hacking-in-2004-ex-employee-says/article534295/ , and http://business.financialpost.com/2012/02/25/nortel-hacked-to-pieces/.

for yourself and co-workers will put your company ahead of the crooked, Chinese curve.

Here are some recommendations:

- follow all the usual and correct internet security practices yourself

- share the internet security rules with co-workers if management doesn't

- talk to your Human Resource department and recommend that it offers: [3]

    o Security education and training for all employees to help them at home and at work

    o Convince them to find a trainer who will make it interesting

- ask if the company is making use of outside "penetration testers" or ethical hackers (these are people you hire to break into your company to test security policy)

CORPORATIONS BEHAVING BADLY

In 1993, British Airways (BA) hacked into Virgin Atlantic.[4] What they did was considered a violation of the Data Protection Act, and possibly the Computer MisUse Act too, but those were the early days of hacking. There was no way to actually get BA in trouble because the penalties for doing these bad things were not clearly defined. However, this has changed dramatically in the last 20 years. Hacking other businesses without their permission – unless you live in China – will result in fines and possibly a prison

---

3 I have worked with and provided training to many large companies. Most IT departments lack the funds to provide cybersecurity training. I believe human resources departments should fund this as it's an employee safety issue and a morale booster if it includes protection for employees at home.

4 http://www.independent.co.uk/news/uk/battle-of-the-airlines-computer-hacking-of-flight-details-was-illegal-british-airways-ran-a-complex-covert-operation-to-steal-customers-from-richard-bransons-virgin-atlantic-1478009.html

term. So no matter what, don't ever, ever, *ever* get roped into being any part of a plan to breach the security of another organization. You will end up in jail, and your family will miss you.

There are two exceptions to this: one is when the hacking is requested by the *hackee*. This is called penetration testing, and companies will pay good money to see how quickly you can defeat their security.[5] If you know someone who loves or lives to hack, this is the job for them.

The second exception has been already covered: you can move to China. There, you can make a comfortable living by selling anything valuable you are able to steal to the government. The government prefers its hackers to freelance so they can deny actually employing them. But it relies on hackers to steal the secrets like the ones Huawei has been using to succeed (the government is heavily connected to Huawei).

DON'T BE *THAT* GUY (OR GAL)

In 2011, nine people who worked for a company earning over $700 million in revenue (with 25,000 total employees) received an email with an infection in it. The email was cleverly disguised as a communication from a party the nine people knew, and it contained a PDF file, something they were used to receiving. All nine emails were caught by the company spam filter. The security policy at this company was clear: no one is supposed to retrieve an email that the system considers spam without clearance from IT. Of the nine employees, one broke protocol and retrieved the email from his spam folder.

When he opened the PDF, there was no observable blip. Often when an infection occurs, something happens on your system – it crashes or hangs or does something else which would alert most people to call their IT department. But in this case there was no slowdown in system response or any other sign of the infection that

---

5 I predict that within 10 years households will receive "cybersecurity testing" services as well.

had just launched in the background. It was months before the infection was discovered and cured. The total financial damage was estimated at $71 million.[6]

WHO IS LIABLE?

None of us want to be that guy, and yet any of us could be.[7] Spam filters are not infallible – so we check them. He obviously thought he was doing the right thing, but he violated the security policy. In U.S. courts, so far this doesn't present a huge problem to the individual since employees are not considered liable for these lapses unless it's malicious.[8] But at some point, companies will do more than simply fire the individual. It's likely that soon "careless security conduct" will carry a fine at the minimum, if not a punitive award by a civil court.

WHEN WE LIKE THE JOB

Not following security protocol is an accepted cause for "termination of employment," whether it's careless or malicious. For this reason, when there are policies that "no one follows," be careful. You may end up being a scapegoat for everyone else. If a break-in occurs because of something you did wrong, it doesn't matter whose footsteps you were following. While it's possible you could get somewhere with a legal case, it would most likely depend upon other employees admitting that they, too, made mistakes. Will they give up their jobs to support your story?

In a perfect world, you want your employer's security policies to make sense. If they don't, and it's impossible to follow them, it could be a case where someone in management is trying to avoid blame for a future breach. The manager's defense would

---

6 Guess what country the hackers were from? Here's a hint: they were after military blue prints. That's right, China!

7 He was up against some of the best hackers the world, and by the time they got to him they had already gained access to some of the network. He only helped them with their last step: onto the super confidential system which contained military blueprints.

8 As in the cases where ex-employees hack into networks to perpetuate damage, steal secrets or cause other mayhem.

be that rules were in place but employees were negligent. In such a situation the Columbo[9] investigative technique "please help me understand…" works best. No need to flat out tell your IT guys that it's a dumb rule which 90% of people don't follow. Try to have a reasonable conversation about other options and suggest they check to see who is following which rules.

One last bit of advice for the employee of the large company: follow the rules from Chapters 8 and 9 for household Internet security and do your best not to take infections to work. Also, if you suspect any kind of breach or infection while using a company laptop at home, make sure you let your IT people know as soon as possible. And finally, always assume your activities are monitored.

This wraps up my security advice for the employee of the large company. The only really comforting news about Fortune 1000 companies is that once they are infected, it usually takes a while for them to fail, so maybe you'll have time to find a new job. Also, a few of them really do pay attention to their security. Just not enough.[10]

FOR THE SMALL BUSINESS OR THE NONPROFIT

There are whole libraries filled with books on security solutions for businesses. There is also a ton of free education about those technologies on the Internet. I couldn't hope to cover that material in just one chapter – my intention is only to get you started by covering the absolute basics.

The first and most important fact for you to know is one that is often over looked.

The most valuable thing you can do to protect your business is completely free.

---

9 Columbo was a television detective (played by Peter Falk) in a series dating back to 1968. Columbo had a distinctive trait of behaving in a befuddled manner and uttering phrases to suspects like, "gosh, can you help me understand how someone could throw themselves out *this* window?" essentially helping suspects implicate themselves and divulge more clues.

10 You'll know how seriously your company takes its security by noticing if it offers any cybercrime education.

This is because small businesses are in the same situation as most homes: they suffer desperately from a lack of knowledge about cybercriminals and how they operate. Remember the biggest problem in security, the people? Whether it's for kids or employees, all we need to do is teach them what to do, how to do it, and why to do it. Then we need to follow through with them until they succeed.

EMPLOYEE EDUCATION

One of the most wonderful things about education is that – because of the Internet, yay! – it can be very cheaply provided.[11] An employee who is motivated to pay attention is the next thing we need. How do we get that?

One way to secure the interest of employees is to teach them how to safer at home first (all Appendixes), because a lot of the principles are the same. Once they grasp those fundamentals – which will also keep them from bringing viruses to work with them – it's time to talk to them about the additional losses that can jeopardize a business or charity:

- The negative impact of telling customers their private information was hacked
    o Loss of customers (revenue)

    o Loss of trust in the brand

    o Being sued for any damage that occurs as a result of the breach

Hopefully, at this point employees are both receptive and interested. This makes it a good time to augment what we have already learned about managing passwords so that it works in the workplace.

---

11 See Appendix G for some inexpensive education ideas.

PASSWORD HELL

Passwords are an area of huge weakness for businesses. It only takes a few slip ups for your most critical secrets (or the donor database) to fall into the wrong hands. The single most important thing you can do, after having good anti-malware, is to make sure you have a system for changing passwords and keeping track of those changes. At home, if we are lucky, we can use the same password and user name on our checking account for 20 years. But this would be highly unusual at a business. Changes in personnel, software, hardware, (etc.) mean that passwords need to change as well. If they don't, we already have at least as many security holes as the number of people who have left or moved to other jobs.

Most companies make mistakes in this area, and sometimes they are multi-million dollar mistakes. They may leave a default password on their router so that anyone can break in, or they may neglect to change the passwords even after someone who knows it has been fired. They may not be tracking the fact that executives or administrators who had special access have left the company. You can start looking at this problem by asking how long each password has been in use.

ANGRY EXES

Also, remember how we discussed the sophisticated organization of cybercrime these days? That now means virtually anyone can sell any valuable data which they can steal. They do this by reaching out to the underground cybercrime network. So an employee or ex-employee who has (or had) access to customer records, employee records, trade secrets, banking passwords, or anything else your company doesn't want falling into the wrong hands – these are the people who should be monitored most closely.

There is also a security rule which says: only provide the information which is absolutely necessary to the people who absolutely need it to do their jobs. Expect them to explain why, and expect the explanation to make sense. This goes against the conventional wisdom which said, "once a person is a Director or a vice president (VP), he or she would never hurt the company so give that individual passwords to every system." But, in fact, just because someone was promoted, there's no reason he or she should have access to information or records which is not needed for his or her job. Trouble-shooting a breach becomes more difficult the larger the pool of suspects – or negligent employees – becomes.

In case you have qualms about monitoring employees because it trespasses upon their privacy, consider this: employees are not going to be there to bail you out when you are sued by a customer whose records were stolen. If the incident which occurred is the employee's fault, they will escape liability but you won't. Your best defense will be that you took "reasonable precautions." Monitoring is very reasonable, and there are many ways to do it. If all you care about is who is accessing certain systems and when, you can find software that will log that information for you. And as long as none of your employees presume that they have privacy – you will help them understand they don't – there's nothing to violate.

If you have passed along what you have learned so far to fellow workers and associates, about now you will be in the same situation as someone trying to manage the Internet security of a household of people. If you are monitoring them, you will know who is following the rules and when. Now it's time to think about keeping them motivated and interested.

KEEPING IT ALL GOING

Getting back to my promise to "get you started," the following is a good set of starter steps for a small business or nonprofit:

1.   Be sure you have strong antivirus products on every computer (not the free stuff)[12]

---

12 There are organizations which test anti-virus software and make the results public. Two of these that are independent (so presumably unbiased) are AV Test and AV Comparative. You can see how anti-virus brands perform against one another at: http://www.av-test.org/en/home/ and http://www.av-comparatives.org/

2. Be sure you have updated all passwords (hardware, software, banking logins, etc.)

3. Be sure any wireless networks are secure (require a code to use; change it if it's too widely known)

4. Set up an all-hands meeting and make copies of the core set of rules (select the appropriate Appendix or Appendixes)

5. Distribute the rules to all employees
   a. Offer employees the rules for personal safety; also – it's always better if their homes are cyber-secure, too

6. Encourage discussion, questions, and suggestions

7. Enlist a cybercrime security volunteer from within the company. It shouldn't cost more than a $25 Starbucks gift card to entice someone into taking this role.

The above actions list should get you going. In a perfect world, the cybersecurity volunteer will take 15 minutes a month or a quarter to find an article about recent cybercrime or an interesting breach (preferably with a pithy moral at the end of the story) and circulate it to everyone. [13] If necessary, rotate the position until you find someone with a passion for cybersecurity. Suggest additional education via conference or webinar as you consider increasing his or her responsibilities.

A FEW LAST WORDS FOR NONPROFITS

This should be a much more common practice than it is: anyone giving a big check to a church or a school should ask for a review of their cybersecurity protocol. It's only reasonable to request a

---

13 One easy place to search for relevant cybersecurity news is: www.threatpost.com

conversation with the IT manager and also one or more employees (or volunteers) about cyber safety. The last thing anyone wants is for donations to be siphoned off by cybercriminals. Large donors have every right to stipulate that certain security measures be adhered to in order for a nonprofit to receive funds. If necessary, take the lead, establish a set of policies and put training in place.

CHAPTER 11

Cyber Terrorists and Cyber Spies – They're Everyone's Problem

> **FACT BOX:** Definitions of Cyber Terrorism usually include an aspect of physical violence. But "Economic Cyber Warfare" can endanger us just as much. Currently the U.S. economy is being stripped of billions of dollars a year as companies go bankrupt when their secrets are stolen and as the money from cyber-thefts leaves the country. This hemorrhaging of money and jobs is capable of further crippling the U.S. economy if not controlled or stopped.

We've all heard about the threat of cyber terrorism. Most of us have seen a movie or two where the theme is at least partially played out. Few people, however, realize that just like the theme of the movie *Die Hard III* – (where a group takes control of a city until a ransom is paid)– such a scenario is easily possible. And some of this has already (albeit, quietly) – happened in the United States.[1] So what can we do to prepare ourselves? How can we protect the ones we love? And what would an attack look like anyway? Let's start by taking a look at the difference between cyber criminals and cyber terrorists.

---

1 Details later in this chapter.

First of all, there's not a lot of agreement on the exact definition of a cyber terrorist.[2] The FBI calls cyber terrorism:

> "a premeditated, politically motivated attack against information, computer systems, computer programs, and data **which results in violence** against **non-combatant** targets by sub-national groups or clandestine agents."

Whew, those are a lot of words. Clearly by the FBI's definition, the villains don't have to be from another country as long as they are targeting us "non-combatants" (civilians). If the target is military to military, like their troops against ours, that's considered cyber war. But it also sounds like if we are held hostage by a group of people who threaten to turn off a power grid they hacked into, as long as they are "politically motivated" and violent, they are cyber terrorists. What if they just demand a nuclear warhead? Or a million dollars? A lot of us would still consider them terrorists.

A somewhat broader definition goes like this:

> "The use of computers and information technology to cause severe disruption or widespread fear in society."

In other words, if some group calling itself American Anarchists hack into a local hospital and threaten to shut it down unless we pay them a million dollars, they are cyber terrorists, not ordinary hoodlums. Just like "cyber crime" the distinction is that they are committing "terrorist acts" and using computer systems as an essential component of the attack. So for the purpose of this discussion, I'm using the broader definition. Whether these bad boys do it for money or politics probably won't matter when it's happening in our neighborhood.

---

2 Merriam-Webster says: "terrorist activities intended to damage or disrupt vital computer systems." Since "terrorism" is defined as "the systematic use of terror as a means of coercion," these acts need not be violent and also not necessarily involve the use of computers (i.e., hacking) to damage or disrupt them. So blowing up computers would be cyber terrorism by this definition.

All of this sounds pretty scary. But a lot of scary things lose their fright-power if we can get close enough to at least look under the bed. Let's start with two questions:

- What is the worst thing that could happen?

- What computer-based systems are so critical to our well-being that we would suffer greatly if they were hacked into and halted?

As we already know, the list of software-dependent systems we rely upon is staggering. Technology is deeply integrated into our transportation systems (metro, trains, flight radar, etc.), hospitals, stadiums, power grids, and water supplies. Obviously it would be extremely inconvenient, uncomfortable and possibly life threatening if any of these were halted for any length of time. It would be tough to get to work, to school or otherwise carry on our usual routines, and communication would be halted as cellular networks failed from overload and computers ran short of battery life.

But wait – is all this really so much different than what we have dealt with for centuries? Doesn't infrastructure shut down look very much like an earthquake to Californians, a tornado to Texans or a killer snowstorm to Minnesotans? For the most part it does. If we don't have a plan for this kind of disaster already, we've all at least thought about putting a kit together. We know we'll have to go for a few days without: power, water, gas, and TV, and we'll run short on food and batteries. So here's my suggestion: use this threat as an incentive to finally put that disaster-preparedness box together. Then let's slap another piece of duct tape next to the one which says, "Earthquake Kit" or "Hurricane Kit" which says, "In case of cyber terrorist attack too" and we and our families will be relatively safe from the worst that can occur to us physically in case of such a threat.

What about the nonphysical? Some people say an attack can only be called "cyber warfare" when it is accompanied by bombs, guns, or tanks. Others say that any nation state that engages in an attack upon another nation state, using computers to attack other computers, is conducting cyber warfare. The big difference between this and cybercrime is that when it comes to the typical cybercriminal, it's every man for him- or herself. Cybercriminals don't belong to a union, and they have no unified agenda. They also only commit as much in the way of resources as they think the prize is worth. They don't have deep pockets to invest in long software development cycles for complex techniques which might not work out.

UTOPIA

But what if we were the leaders of a large country that desires to dominate the world? Suppose we have a huge amount of control over our citizens. We set economic policy, so we decide who earns how much for which jobs. We also censor all the news they get – we helpfully slant it to so they can better appreciate us. We have control over military forces which instantly and effectively suppress protests at our command.

Now that you have the picture, here's the question: Why *wouldn't* we train hackers to steal secrets from other more innovative countries? Is there any reason not to? After all, it's part of our job to make the nation prosperous. If we don't steal information that enriches us and weakens our competitors we are not doing our jobs. And if we are squeamish about such cutthroat tactics, there are lots more comrades willing to step up and take our place.

We also have the best and the brightest hackers of a vast nation at our disposal. Of course, our top hackers will be rewarded with a nice lifestyle so there will be no shortage of motivated applicants. Up to now, all of this is a good description of China.

We could quibble a bit about the exact number of cyber spies China has, but the FBI says they have 180,000.[3] That's a lot. Surely

---

3 This is a good article about some of the details, although it's not much of a secret any more: http://www.thedailybeast.com/articles/2010/01/13/chinas-secret-cyber-terrorism.html .

the United States have some as well, but there's a big difference in terms of what China's focus is.

To be even-handed about this, *most* countries who believe they have enemies by now have cyber-spy teams trying to hack their opponents' military targets and extract secrets. It's par for the course in a world that believes that "the best defense is a good offense"[4]. But China is special in that the government, in addition to being entrusted with protection and manipulation of its citizens, is very heavily involved with every successful business. There's no real line drawn in China between what we would call private industry and government coffers. Further, the Chinese aren't known to be great innovators but they are terrific copiers, and they make lots of money copying at lower costs. So why not steal plans from a place that's known for spawning interesting ideas? The fact is, we (security people and law enforcement) have been able to trace many attacks back to Chinese soil.

PRETTY PLEASE...

We Americans have this peculiarly puritanical idea that if we look someone straight in the eye and ask a question, he or she won't lie to us. We believe if we ask clearly and firmly, then for the sake of honor, we will be told the truth. It's a quaint idea, but surely out of place in this situation.

Astonishingly, the media continue to ask for, and print, Chinese denials. But Communist Chinese leadership consists of people who have killed their own students to quash rebellions... remember Tiananmen Square? Asking whether or not the Chinese government is hacking U.S. businesses and *believing the answer* is nonsensical. If they are motivated to hack us, they should be equally motivated to lie to us about it. And remember the chapter on trust? Shouldn't people (or governments) have to prove their credibility before we trust them enough to include them in the

---

4 A phrase that originated with Chairman Mao.. It should go without saying, but there are many admirable things about Chinese culture, including its adeptness at war. Communism...not so much.

conversation? "Innocent until proven guilty" is a great way to run a free country, and maybe a household, but it ought to stop at certain borders.

SO WHOM CAN WE TRUST?

No government can afford to be careless about its own survival, even the U.S. government (which is supposedly "for the people, by the people"). For that reason, it's naïve for us to expect to get the whole truth about anything. There have been enough times in history when the public went off "half-cocked" with a little bit of dangerous information; our government is well aware that if we got upset enough, we might storm Washington with our pitchforks and our constitutionally-guaranteed, semi-automatic assault rifles. It could get ugly. And we'd be sorry after we did it, because most of us really just want to be left alone to our own personal, peaceful pursuit of happiness. So no wonder our government officials are cautious about what they tell us. Fortunately we have Hacktivists to keep them honest.

Here's a good example of what the bureaucrats aren't telling us. It's easier to see it based on a timeline:

****

In **January 2008**, a CIA analyst stated at a conference that **utility companies** "outside the U.S." had been **blackmailed after hackers** gained control of their systems. At the same conference, a guy who argues that cybercrime is over-hyped called it "pure urban myth." Hmmm, maybe he really believed it was hype. No one (outside of the field of cybersecurity) can blame him because that was two- years before the discovery of Stuxnet. Stuxnet is an incredibly sophisticated piece of malware that does a fantastic job of taking control of the SCADA computer platform and handing it over to hackers. Unfortunately for us,

SCADA is used worldwide to run all kinds of utility companies from nuclear power plants to water utilities. When it was discovered in 2010, it had been operational for at least two years.[5]

In **June of 2008** there was another report, this one specifically about **hackers being responsible for power outages**. A senior security expert who had worked with the government for years said that a power outage which affected 50 million homes in August 2003 across New York, Michigan, Ohio, and parts of Canada was the result of Chinese hackers. Another outage in Florida in 2008 was also blamed on a Chinese cyber intruder.[6]

After the above article was printed, there were no U.S. Government denials. I'm betting that the denial policy hadn't been invented yet. However, the government must have decided it needed to control the possibility of public panic (remember the pitchforks!) because here's what happened next (in 2011):

November 17, 2011, it is reported that **hackers destroyed a water pump** at an "undisclosed water utility in an undisclosed city" in the United States.

Later the same day, Department of Homeland Security says it isn't so.

November 18, 2011, a hacker who is furious that the Department of Homeland Security (DHS) is denying that his hacks occurred, posts screen shots of the details of his second attack. It was conducted against the City of South Houston, Texas. He also wrote:

"I dislike, immensely, how the DHS tend to downplay how absolutely F—D the state of national infrastructure is," the post stated. "I've also seen various people doubt the possibility an attack like this could be done."

---

5 http://www.theregister.co.uk/2008/01/21/scada_threat_warning/
6 http://www.theregister.co.uk/2008/06/02/chinese_blamed_us_power_outage/

Then on **November 23, 2011**, in keeping with the new denial policy, the FBI stated, "there's no evidence of cyber intrusion" upon (the originally reported facility) a water plant in Springfield, Illinois.

****

Okay, sure, FBI people. But most of us have heard this before or we've been through it with our kids. My youngest son Matt once said, indignantly, "I *didn't* hit [my brother] in the face with the ball!" But when pressed, he admitted, "Okay, so I hit the ball. Then *the ball* hit Nick in the face."

The famous Stuxnet infection didn't occur by "cyber intrusion" initially. First hackers had to get their malware into the system. Since nuclear facilities are not connected to the internet, hackers left infected thumb drives lying around, which employees picked up. The workers did what most people do; they plugged the drives into their computers to see what was on them. So technically speaking, the FBI denial could be correct ("there's no evidence of cyberintrusion") even if the utility plants were hacked.

I have to guess –or, maybe "hope" is more like it – that the government has been re-thinking its denial policy since a lot of hackers can't help wanting to prove their handiwork. And really, hats off to the Houston Utility Hacker for making his point this way…and trying to alert the public.[7]

MUM'S NOT THE WORD

But if you think our government isn't warning us about Internet security at all, it's only because we, the people, haven't been listening. Apparently when they are *really* concerned, they

---

7 Here's one link that will take you to a list of all of these articles: http://search.theregister.co.uk/?q=water+utility+hack+US

are willing to talk about some of these things. Unfortunately, cybersecurity topics (since we haven't been focused on them enough) can easily get lost in all the other news going on. The government issued its most blunt statement on this topic *ever* just a few weeks before the 2012 presidential election. So are we to blame if we were too distracted to notice?

Here's what they said: In October of 2012, the U.S. House Intelligence Committee recommended that several high-profile Chinese manufacturers of routers and telecommunications infrastructure equipment be banned from doing business in the United States. The committee members warned the Canadian government not to allow Huawei to bid on deals to build Internet and telecom infrastructure for fear that the equipment may have ways to "spy" on users. The Committee went on to say that U.S. businesses using products by these companies additionally should:

> "find another vendor if you care about your intellectual
> property; if you care about your consumers' privacy and
> you care about the national security of the United States
> of America."[8]

If you believe (as I and most people in IT security do) our government, then what else can be learned from this? Is there a way to apply our government's warning to your own security? Do you know whether your email is currently running across Chinese routers?

The answers to these questions can easily lead us to consider the ideal function of government in the civilized (non-dictatorial) world. How has government helped us in the past? As cynical as we can be about politics, our government definitely provides some critical functions. At least for every one of us who appreciate opportunity, freedom, and safety. Without an organized government, we would have no interstate freeways, no Internet,

---

8 http://www.techradar.com/us/news/phone-and-communications/mobile-phones/huawei-and-zte-should-be-banned-from-us-says-intelligence-committee-1102651. Here's another article about the Chinese threat: http://www.theregister.co.uk/2011/12/24/china_cybercrime_underground_analysis/.

and no FEMA to help absorb the pain of national disasters. And, there's something else most Americans take for granted: we can count on Uncle Sam to nationalize certain safety requirements for us and our families.

An interview published December 24, 2012, with Bruce Schneier[9] (a heavyweight in the security industry) focuses on water. He says that we turn on the tap and trust that what comes out is safe to consume. Why? Because for a very long time now, the United States government has regulated the safety of tap water.

(As an aside, how would you feel about drinking tap water someone sent you from Somalia? In case that happens, here's a tip: Somalia is number one on the list of countries with not enough drinkable water and thousands of people die there every year from drinking contaminated water.)[10]

Schneier goes on to say that we can't trust (profit-driven) companies to make the best choices about our security because sometimes the best choice is expensive. And since the Internet is comprised of so many elements **invisible** to those of us using it, and **no single one of us has much power**, the Internet is an ideal place for government oversight.

The government's admonishment about not using Chinese routers makes Schneier's point perfectly. If one of us calls our Internet service provider and asks: "what kind of routers are you using to route my email?" The customer service team at Comcast or AT&T won't even know how to respond to the question. So maybe someone else, like a government agency with our best interests at heart, should be asking for us.

This could work in the same way that the government regulates and oversees other things like aircraft inspections, trucking, and the building industry. Certain safety standards are agreed upon and compliance is measured. With our protective Big Brother

---

9 The interview was by Adam Adam Popescu for *readwrite* magazine http://readwrite.com/2012/12/24/schneier-on-digital-feudalism-cyberterrorism-and-zombie-sopa

10 Go to http://water.org/ to see how we can help (actor Matt Damon is a co-founder)

establishing "minimum acceptable security" for us, we would be able to pick safe Internet security providers with confidence. (Or maybe we pick the cheapest company with the worst Internet hygiene, but at least then we know not to conduct our online banking across that network!)

Here are two other ways the government could help us:

- Provide a rating of the level of "security commitment" of the most popular software being used today. This would be based upon the attention companies give to fixing major security flaws. By example, in this category, Microsoft would get an "A". But even just a year ago cybersecurity companies would have given Apple an "F".[11] It didn't mean we wouldn't buy Apple's products, only that installing additional security software after purchase was even more important. But today Apple is finally doing a reasonable job of responding to security issues (perhaps a "B minus").

- Jeremiah Grossman of White Hat Security says, "Hack Yourselves." He is suggesting that businesses hack themselves to self-test for security flaws. It's a great idea for individuals, too, except most of us lack the skills. So how about regulating companies who offer this service to households? Like a smog test, they quickly hack our security (and test our Internet service provider) once every two years and give us a score. They could also let us know how to make it better. These companies should be regulated like car mechanics, where the

---

11 Not to pick on Apple: I love them for the same reasons everyone else does (cool products). When Apple was small and niche compared to Windows, it didn't have to worry about security, since the payout for attacking Macs was small. But as the Apple platforms have grown in popularity, the company has not changed its attitude. This is irresponsible. Even with the discovery of massive botnets of Macs (recently, 700K systems in one botnet) Apple still ignored security issues to the point of not even responding to security experts who attempt to notify the company of flaws. Here's an example: Jeremiah Grossman informed them of a security flaw in June 2010. Here is the link to his blog about it: http://news.softpedia.com/news/Apple-Disables-AutoFill-in-iOS-6-Safari-Without-Warning-313899.shtml

government provides a GoodHackMaster Seal of Approval.[12]

GETTING THE GREEN

In this time of massive government deficits, you must be asking, how would we fund this? Well, here are two ideas:

First, we take everyone who is currently fulfilling a role providing security-for-show and we re-deploy them to this new group, where their work would actually benefit us.

For example, consider all the Transportation Security Administration (TSA) agents at the airport. At airport security screening points, we see lots of people parading around in uniforms, frowning at scanners, and patting down coat pockets as if checking for firearms. All of this probably reassures some people, but there is ample evidence showing that it's so ineffective it will at most catch the occasional dimwitted or mentally ill miscreant.

Since it's obviously quite expensive, why does the government do these things? Bruce Schneier calls it "security theatre." They are putting on a show for us, and he coined the term to describe all those things done to make citizens feel more secure even though the measures themselves don't actually help. Another great example occurred back in the 1950s: teachers at elementary schools helped kids practice ducking under their desks to prepare in case of nuclear bomb detonation. At the time, the atom bomb was a scary new threat which most people did not understand. The top brass had seen the simulations and knew desk-ducking was a useless exercise, but providing the public with a ritual to practice "just in case" probably helped everyone sleep at night.

A decade has passed since 9/11. Maybe we are ready now to let airport security theatre go the way of desk-ducking and shift the resources to a place where they can do some real good.

---

12 Note to businesses— companies should then say, "unless your Home Hackabilty Quotient is in this range, you can't use your laptop on your home wireless", etc. This could close a lot of security holes for employers.

Second, there could be some self-funding. We pay for vehicle registration and for our own smog tests. Building departments collect fees for inspections. Why couldn't there be a nominal registration fee collected to ensure everyone complies with some measure of cybersecurity? (That's it for my funding ideas: I respectfully leave the rest of the details to the bureaucrats to figure out!)

THE TOLL IF WE DON'T

The biggest and most compelling reason the government should step in *now* is because we *cannot* afford the alternative. If they don't act soon, we will be past the point from which we can recover. We can't know right now how many other companies – like Nortel or RSA – are on the verge of collapse because their ideas have been copied and strategies rendered useless. Just a few multinationals could easily mean the loss of a million jobs and billions of dollars. Can the United States afford this?

Our biggest security problem isn't figuring out whether there's going to be the cyber terrorist equivalent of an 8.0 earthquake in San Francisco next Tuesday. It's the fact that slowly, steadily, and terribly, our intellectual capital is leaking out of the country. These are our core assets, and they represent an economic value of staggering proportion. Such losses have the ability to permanently change our future for the worse. After enough ideas have been stolen, executed elsewhere, and manufactured to be sold more cheaply, and too many of our business strategies are leap-frogged at every turn – we will be unable to fund innovation any longer. We will cease to lead the world in anything. Except maybe being the nicest of all the Nice Guys.

WHAT CAN WE DO?

Isn't it great that we can reach Congress with email these days? We don't even have to buy stamps. That's where this kind of change starts. Send an email to your congresswomen and congressmen to let them know that you are concerned about the safety of the

Internet infrastructure, since we are all forced to rely on it. Then locate a source (or two) – security bloggers or newsletters or ezines with opinions you trust – and make sure that these trusted sources are in agreement with whatever your representative comes up with as a solution.

The reason you should have someone from security provide a stamp of approval is:

a.) we all know better than to fully trust politicians (right?)

b.) very few politicians have an in-depth understanding of the technology basics, like the fact that security *always* requires giving something else up. And, yes, there is such a thing as "too secure" (remember the alligators and the moat)

Other than that:

o   Be *twice* as ready for a natural disaster (this will cover you for cyber terrorism too – don't forget the water)[13]

o   Vote when necessary

o   Don't take safety for granted

I hate to end this chapter on such a somber note, but this stuff is pretty important. Now let's cover one last very interesting group of hackers you will be hearing more and more about.

---

13 For those of you who don't have the time to put a kit together, these can be purchased. Try places in Utah especially: as I learned from a co-worker who is Mormon, they believe every family should be prepared to be off-the-grid for a year.

CHAPTER 12

Vigilantes on the Internet - Hacktivists to Love...or Hate

> **FACT BOX:** Vigilantes are people who take action to uphold moral codes without the legal authority to do so. They engage in this activity because they believe existing mechanisms are ineffective or inefficient. In the case of "hacktivists," although their actions are often illegal, the fact remains that their basic assumption that the police and other intelligence agencies are often too over-whelmed to assist victims and render justice is correct.

Hacktivists are featured more and more frequently in the news. Because they are a cybercrime element, we should discuss them. As I write this for example, a group of hacktivists are at the center of a rape case in Ohio.[1] Expect to see many more such cases where evidence is hacked and posted to help a perceived victim as time goes on.

The term "hacktivist" is a combination of the word "hacker" and "activist." They hack on behalf of causes they believe in. If you agree with their cause, you might like what they do. There may be other times you won't. Occasionally, two different groups of hacktivists are on opposing sides of an issue, and they attack each

---

1 The case in Steubenville, Ohio of the Big Red football team.

other. And, like any organization, there can be discord within the ranks, including disagreements about which tactics to use.

As a private citizen, you are unlikely to be hurt by hacktivists directly, but they may attack companies, or groups, or individuals you know. They especially get into trouble when they hack the FBI. Because they are such a powerful force, it is helpful to know who they are, what they do, and what motivates them.

Hacktivists have an interesting, if sometimes frightening, objective: to use their hacking skill to correct certain perceived wrongs in the world. Another term for this is "Internet vigilantism." When hacktivists share the details of someone's bad behavior with law enforcement, it may be called "cyber-snitching". But to those of us in anti-cybercrime, the catch phrase that works best is hacktivism.

Some hacktivists work alone. For larger-scale, multipoint attacks, these individuals connect online to form a group. Each person agrees to certain tasks, and along the way other hackers may join (if they like the cause). When the project has been fully executed, they may disband until the next attack. A group of hacktivists who have worked together on multiple projects, or who come together with a defined longer-term objective, often name themselves. One of the most famous of these groups called Anonymous, and there's even a documentary about Anonymous called *We Are Legion*.

COME ONE, COME ALL

Hacktivism is very inclusive. If you are a hacker with time on your hands and the right level of skill, and you feel sympathetic towards the goal of a given group, you are welcome to join.[2] It's not quite as easy as that – and will probably get harder – since some hacktivists have turned on one another when threatened with jail time. But that is essentially how it works. Sometimes these

---

2 Hackers who have professional security certifications and/or jobs in cybersecurity or law enforcement are restricted from doing anything illegal. If they do and they are caught, they risk not just jail but also professional censure and the loss of their jobs and certifications.

groups actually take requests from the public for causes or targets to attack.

BAD BOYS (AND GIRLS)

For the most part, hacktivists are considered criminals by the cybersecurity community. This is because a lot of what they do is illegal. They also tend to upset law enforcement at all levels, various governments, and the CEOs of target companies. So, they are universally considered outlaws.

But there is one simple argument in favor of the existence of hacktivists: the world is not fair. People do terrible things and get away with it. And we human beings have a deep craving for justice. Witness our multimillion dollar action movie industry with movies like *Jack Reacher* and *Safe* if you have any doubt. We love to see the bad guy "get what was coming" to him in the end. And more often than not, payback happens outside the usual civilized channels like cops and court.

If you're not sure that there's anything these outlaws could do which you *personally* might cheer about, let me share a few examples of their work:

CAT ABUSE

In February 2009, a video clip was posted on YouTube showing a domestic cat named Dusty being beaten and tortured by a 14-year old boy calling himself "Timmy." After 30,000 views the clip was removed by YouTube. But members of the 4chan hacktivist group learned of the clip and investigated. They were able to figure out who Timmy really was (extrapolating from his user name and other video details) along with the cameraman (both juveniles). The hacktivists provided this information to the police department where the boys lived and both boys were arrested. Although under 18, the courts say that punishment could include "psychological counseling, court monitoring until they turn 18, community service to provide restitution for treatment of animals, and/or placement in court custody."

Dusty survived the abuse, thankfully, and was placed in the care of a local vet. Is it possible that 4chan halted in his tracks a future Jeffrey Dahmer[3]?

PROTECTING KIDS

There are also hacktivists who go after child predators[4]:

Members of the hacktivist group Anonymous have been credited for seeking out pedophiles and collaborating with law enforcement. In 2007, a 53-year old man, Chris Forcand, was trolling the web for minors to have sex with. Members of Anonymous posed as a girl and turned the ensuing messages and screen shots over to Toronto police who promptly arrested him.

In late 2011, Anonymous launched Operation Darknet[5] that targeted websites trafficking in child porn. In addition to shutting down a server called Freedom Hosting[6] identified by Anonymous as the "largest distributor of child porn on the Internet,". The hacktivists were also able to obtain the personal details of more than 1,100 pedophiles that they made available to the FBI and Interpol.[7]

Members of another group called Alt.Hackers.Malicious also took credit for dozens of arrests and convictions of child predators. They are best known for breaking into the website of an organization promoting sex between adult males and young boys (NAMBLA) and providing membership information along with incriminating emails to law enforcement. Their work led to several arrests and convictions for child sexual abuse.

---

3 Jeffrey Dahmer, one of the worst serial killers of all time started with the killing and torture of animals.
4 Specific details are courtesy of Wikipedia (although confirmed with other sources).
5 See glossary for full "darknet" definition, but these originated to assist people living in authoritarian countries that censor the internet. Unfortunately they have also been used to hide the identities of child molesters.
6 See "Denial of Service" attack in the glossary if you'd like to know how they did this.
7 If you are wondering how they do this without being caught or identified, they paste the information into Pastebin (see glossary for full definition) and invite law enforcement to view it.

Of course, not every hacktivist activity is in the defense of animals or children. In 2012, Uganda proposed legislation that would put all homosexuals to death. Anonymous hacked into the government's website and among other things they posted a fake letter from the Ugandan Prime Minister to the people. The letter essentially revealed that he had realized how wrong his views were and he begged the Ugandans to forgive him. Most Americans can appreciate the humor in this; it's hard to imagine a country so brutally backwards that it would legally murder its own people, based on their sexual orientation.

Internet censorship is another area Anonymous monitors closely. Sometimes a piece of regulatory legislation will be introduced that threatens to censor the Internet, such as the SOPA or PIPA bills (put forth in 2011, but defeated by early 2012). The bills were meant to address issues of online pirating of games, movies, and music.

Everyone agrees that pirating is a costly problem which should be solved.[8] The challenge is figuring out *how* to solve it without also compromising beloved Internet fundamentals. Wikipedia, along with many other sites, protested by going off-line for a day with this statement on its website: "The U.S. Congress is considering legislation that could fatally damage the free and open Internet." Included were links to members of Congress.

In a stunning upset, both the Senate and the House were deluged by constituents swayed by Google, Wikipedia, and hacktivists. One political analyst called it a "watershed moment" when a free channel of communication (the Internet) could defeat the effect of over $14 million worth of lobbying (the amount spent by entertainment interest groups in the previous year).

Another somewhat-politically-motivated attack involved U.S. Presidential hopeful, Mitt Romney. On, September 4, 2012, a

---

8 Currently the U.S. loses $100 billion a year in royalties and other fees due to illegal pirating.

group of hackers – or hacktivists, you decide[9] – claimed they had gained access to the computers of the accounting firm PwC (PricewaterhouseCoopers) who file Mitt and Ann Romney's tax returns. The hackers said they had obtained copies of every tax return before 2010 (at the time Mitt had refused to release any of these). The hacktivists demanded a million dollars in ransom or they would ensure that the returns were received by all major media outlets. They furnished precise details of how the attack occurred, even down to the physical room the server was in. Supposedly, they had already provided encrypted thumb drives containing the tax returns to various journalists, reporters, and to the Democratic National Committee headquarters. If the ransom was not paid by September 28, the hacktivists said they would provide every thumb drive recipient with a code to unlock the data.

This supposed breach was widely reported on September 5, but PwC denied that the returns were stolen. So is it merely a *huge* coincidence that the Romneys released their returns on September 24? Add to this "coincidence," one more piece of evidence: on October 7, 2012, PricewaterhouseCoopers posted over 10 job openings on dice.com with titles of, "Cybercrime Manager" and "Senior Cybercrime Director."

What happened to Price Waterhouse and Mitt could happen to anyone. If a brilliant hacker wants your stuff, he's probably going to get it. And maybe PwC is just advertising for cybercrime expertise because the "purported" breach made the company realize it was vulnerable.

WHAT ELSE?

If you're a patriot, there's another interesting cause some hacktivists are working on: helping U.S. defense. At least one of these guys isn't concerned about remaining anonymous: Jeff

---

9 If they really thought they might get the ransom, they are ordinary cybercriminals. But if they only asked for ransom in order to spur the disclosure, they had a genuine cause which makes them hacktivists.

Bardin. He lectures about cybercrime and is described by the Los Angeles *Times*[10] as a stout, 54-year-old computer security consultant. But often, he's pretending to be a Canadian man in his twenties who wants to train at a militant camp in Pakistan. This is easy for him because he speaks and writes fluent Arabic.

Bardin used to serve in the Air Force. He is part of a group of hacktivists who spy on Al Qaeda. His specialty is getting into chat rooms and sites where extremists are seeking recruits. Over the last seven years, he has provided the FBI and U.S. military a steady stream of information he found by hacking jihadist websites. Although many officials in the government confirmed the value of Bardin's work, others are concerned about the possibility that military-motivated civilian hacktivists might disrupt existing intelligence operations.

It's not hard to understand that concern: Hacktivists answer to no one, so, of course, their actions might not always synch up with our country's larger defense plans. But it sure sounds like they are doing something which makes a difference. There's another guy who calls himself the Jester.

The Jester is a hacktivist who uses a customized software program that launches DDoS[11] attacks against jihadist websites. But he doesn't stop there. Although many hacktivists defended Wikileaks to the point of attacking sites that stopped supporting Assange's team, the Jester has claimed responsibility for the November 2010 takedown of the WikiLeaks website. He says that by publishing 400,000 classified U.S. military reports from Iraq, Julian Assange and his team put national security at risk. The Jester also claims to have disabled 20 websites associated with the Westboro Baptist Church, an extremist Kansas-based group known

---

10 Link to the article here: http://articles.latimes.com/2012/sep/08/nation/la-na-terror-hacker-20120909
11 Distributed Denial of Service – see glossary for complete definition, but it describes a process of overwhelming a web server so that the website it is hosting becomes unavailable.

for protesting homosexuality. The problem being, these Baptists take their protests to military funerals.[12]

The Jester says (through interviews given by instant messaging) he was a former soldier who served four tours in Afghanistan and elsewhere. He has said he enjoys disrupting terrorist networks, but doesn't want to work for the government (he cited red tape and too many hoops to jump through). In the same way that he went after Wikileaks, the Jester sometimes goes after hacktivists who he believes are "irresponsible" or "childish."

WHO'S SIDE ARE YOU ON?

As you can see, there are as many hacktivist causes as there are points of view. Some will make you want to cheer, others may incite you. Certainly, there are things they do that are controversial. But do take this advice. If you ever get on the bad side of a hacktivist: apologize! And do it quickly. Because no matter how bad it is, believe me, it can get worse.

WAS IT THE ARROGANCE OR THE COPYRIGHT?

The food magazine *Cooks Source* printed an article by blogger Monica Gaudio without her permission in its November 2010 issue. Gaudio learned of the copyright violation and emailed Judith Griggs, the managing editor. Gaudio requested that the magazine both apologize and also donate $130 to the Columbia School of Journalism as payment for using her work. Instead, Gaudio received a letter from Judith Griggs stating that Gaudio should be thanking the magazine for making the piece better and that Gaudio was lucky Griggs bothered to give her credit for writing it at all.

Gaudio went public with these details and online vigilantes took it upon themselves to avenge her. The *Cooks Source* Facebook

---

12 These are the people who carry signs saying, "Thank God for dead soldiers" and say that God is killing US soldiers because they fight for a country that tolerates homosexuality. Perhaps they should move to Uganda.

page was flooded with thousands of angry comments, forcing the magazine's staff to create new pages to escape the protest. A week later the magazine's website was stripped of all content by the staff and shut down. An apology may not have saved *Cooks Source*, but a less arrogant editor might have at least tried.

WATCHDOGS?

When it comes to the most extreme cases of horrid behavior, people are still learning that we live in an age when news travels instantly, often accompanied by video evidence.[13] Internet purveyors – over two billion of them now - are able to gather data and come to conclusions sometimes *moments* after events occur. We can't count on the mainstream press to notice every maimed kitten or pick up every important story. In the aftermath of awful events, which may otherwise go completely unnoticed – is it really such a bad thing for hacktivists to have the underdog's (or cat's, or kid's) back?

If there *is* a place for hacktivists in the world today, that place will be rendered obsolete only when:

1.) Perfect justice exists (people stop getting away with hurting others just because no one knows about it, or the perpetrator is stronger, richer, more connected, etc.).

2.) The Internet is a secure place.

Since neither of these will come to pass any time soon, I think we can count on a steady stream of hacktivist stories with wrongs being righted for a long time to come. Let's just hope that for the most part we agree with the hacktivists' ethics, because – just as with cybercriminals – there's very little we can do to stop them.

---

13 Google the rape case against "Big Red" football players in Steubenville, Ohio to see what I mean. Hacktivists were very involved in bringing visibility to a case which many people feared would be ignored in such a staunch "football town."

CHAPTER 13

Finally: The *Only* Benefit of Cybercrime

FACT BOX: According to John Slye, an industry analyst with the market intelligence firm GovWin, growth in cybersecurity spending in the United States is expected to increase from $9.3 billion in 2011 to $14.1 billion in 2016. "Spending," of course, includes the salaries paid to new employees. Here are the top four anti-cybercrime job markets in order of their expected number of job openings: the San Francisco Bay Area (including Silicon Valley), Boston, Denver, and Maryland. In Maryland alone, in October of 2012, there were over 13,000 active job openings for people with cybercrime expertise.

There is one positive effect of the cybercrime explosion. While the value is small relative to the overall cost of cybercrime, it is worth mentioning because many people can benefit from it.

The effect amounts to a little bit of economic "payback." For all the money cybercriminals suck out of economies worldwide, billions of dollars and probably a hundred thousand jobs are also generated in our fight against it. In the same way that higher crime rates cause us to purchase alarm systems or vote for more police protection, without cybercrime there would be no anti-cybercrime industry. And this rapidly growing, multibillion-dollar industry is capable of supplying the average person with three things:

- Products to make us safer

- Personnel who will implement security for us – for a fee

- Jobs in anti-cybercrime, aka Internet safety

As far as the products themselves go, you already know you need the best anti-malware you can afford. There are additional product suggestions in the appendixes. You've also received plenty of information about ways in which you or members of your household can change to avoid being victimized. So let's take a look at people who can help us as we go about implementing these changes. Quite understandably, when it comes to some of the technical details like securing a router, many people don't want to deal with the details of managing their own security.

HANDLING THE TECHNICAL PART

If you are short on time or you lack technical interest in Internet security, don't let these things stop you from protecting your household: Outsource it. Managing the process can be quite simple. Here are some options to consider:

- Ask friends or neighbors for references for a local computer service company, or check a site with user reviews like Yelp.com

- Find help at your local electronics store. Best Buy has its Geek Squad for example, or try Radio Shack

- Check college campus career centers – pay a student to do it (but check his or her references)

- Use phone service tech support (much, if not all, of what is necessary can be accomplished by giving a technician temporary control of your system)

- Cook a meal or trade other skills to an IT person at the office, and have him or her set up your IT security

Whatever you do, don't let discomfort keep you from moving ahead. Take the appropriate lists of rules from this book's appendixes and give them to your chosen expert.

ENLIST WITH CAUTION

As you consider your options, don't forget the matter of trust. An attractive married woman who works at a multinational high-tech company began to receive threatening letters. Tony, a male friend of hers from work, who had excellent computer and electrical skills, came to the rescue and offered to install security systems at her house. She accepted. Things soon escalated to the point where she received intimate recordings and video of herself from the stalker. It took another two years and a police investigation to learn that Tony himself was the culprit. In the process of setting up her alarm system, he had also installed hidden cameras in her home and spyware on her computer.

In another example from October 2012, a large rent-to-own computer company was sued by a couple in Wyoming after it was discovered that the rental company had been cyber spying (via Webcam) on the couple. Among other things, the camera captured images of them in "intimate moments." Apparently, this was a feature – turning on Webcams without the renters knowing about it – which was used company-wide by all the franchisees as well. The software that allows this is currently installed on over 400,000 computers owned by various computer rental companies in the United States, Canada, and Australia.[1]

WHO ELSE CAN WE COUNT ON?

This may look like a whole new security problem when we have to vet the people who are supposed to help us, but it is an unfortunate requirement. When we have strangers setting up our security, it's a good idea to have the work reviewed by people we

---

1 You can read the details in this article by Information Week: http://www.informationweek.com/security/client/ftc-wrist-slaps-pc-rental-firms-for-spyi/240007967

trust. And like everything in life, the more willing we are to pay attention and be involved, the better. Collect references and for goodness sake, turn off the computer or leave it in the living room when having private conversations. A piece of duct tape over the Webcam is another good policy.

EXPECTING YOUR MATE TO DO IT

As a parent who is also employed in high tech, I can attest to the fact that not everyone who works in a technical field looks forward to spending his or her evenings managing Internet security for the household. It's easy to assume, if your spouse was the one who installed the anti-malware, he or she has taken care of everything else, too. But it's important to check this assumption - don't wait until your bank accounts have been demolished to discover that your partner never got around to implementing the rest of the rules. In the situation where none of the adult members of the household wish to take on the responsibility of Internet safety – back to the solution above – hire someone to do it.

UNCLE SAM

We can't trust in Uncle Sam to fix things for us either. A government that can't even balance its own checkbook isn't likely to put a dent in something as twisted, brilliant, and borderless as cybercrime. Expect it to go the way of the drug war – government officials will make great efforts, do the best they can, and spend lots of money but to little avail. (Although there are some things the government *can* help us with – see Chapter 11 for those ideas.) When the government does apply itself, expect it to be on larger issues like cyber terrorism and cyber warfare, not trying to get back the money citizens have sent to con artists living in other countries, or even to help us get back our hacked 401Ks.

KEEPING CURRENT

After you implement the new rules you will want to stay up to speed on new problems, scams, and cybercrime trends which might affect you and your family. Find a source (or two or three) you trust to provide email updates on the latest cybercrime concerns. Suggestions regarding sources can be found in Appendix G, but new products are constantly being released and reviewed (make sure you are reading unbiased reviews, which aren't only pushing a product!). Another option is to set aside some time every six months to spend an hour browsing sources such as the FBI's Cyber Alerts[2] to see if there's anything new about which household members should be warned. Whether this job falls to you or you appoint someone else as the anti-cybercrime advocate (this could be a paid position for a teen), it is ideal to share this information as broadly as possible among your friends, family, and extended community. There are free tools to help in these efforts too: there are groups like StopThinkConnect and iKeepSafe (both listed in Appendix H), that encourage community outreach. They also provide materials to volunteers at no cost. They do this because we desperately need to get the word out. We need more people doing outreach, whether through casual conversations or concerted educational efforts. Involvement like this – anything from sharing materials with children in a church group to providing a short presentation for senior citizens – is also a good way to help anyone decide if the work is interesting enough to consider as a career.

CAREERS IN CYBERSECURITY

Cybersecurity has expanded so rapidly over such a short period of time that it provides opportunities for people from both ends of the educational spectrum. There are jobs for those who are willing to take one-week courses in "Ethical Hacking" (as an entry level participant in a "penetration testing" company[3]) and those who

---

2 http://www.fbi.gov/scams-safety/e-scams
3 These companies are paid to test cybersecurity by trying to crack it under controlled conditions.

have PhDs in cryptography or mathematics. Without describing all the possible cybersecurity specialties (this is better done in books dedicated to the subject), a very short list includes people who:

- Evaluate security measures
- Investigate cybercrime
- Analyze cyberattacks
- Hack-for-hire (legally)
- Analyze malware
- Teach
- Develop anti-cybercrime products
- Sell and market anti-cybercrime products

In many companies the only requirement to begin training in the area of Internet security is a willingness to step into the role. And like any situation where the demand exceeds the supply, employers are willing to be especially flexible. So it's potentially a great way for people who haven't been previously employed in technology to get involved.

THE FINAL FIVE

In whatever way you care about Internet safety, here are five final rules to keep in mind.

1.) **No one in anti-cybercrime knows it all - don't be afraid to ask for help**. It's impossible to solve problems as complex as cybercrime without the involvement of a lot of experts working issues at the same time, and people who are specialists in one area may know very little about the details of another area.

2.) **The more communication about cybercrime, the better.** If grandma doesn't know about the scam where a rep calls pretending to be Microsoft, or your best friend who just started Internet dating doesn't realize that Webcams are a necessity, they are in very vulnerable positions. These stories need to be shared widely in order to neutralize the threat. Taking this information to the rest of the community – a school, a church, a synagogue, a charity – can ensure people are taking precautions to not infect one another. Everyone needs to be included in cyber-safety training if we are all going to be safe.

3.) **There is always a tradeoff between privacy and security.** The easiest way to judge potential threats is when everything is visible. People resist this idea because they value their privacy, but there will always be tradeoffs between anonymity and safety. The presumption of privacy while using the Internet is unrealistic. Whether the people "listening" are hackers, government agencies, or an employer, it is far safer to presume we have no privacy. And, of course, because they are so easily victimized, young children shouldn't have Internet privacy at all.

4.) **The burden is upon each of us to ensure security for ourselves and everyone else we care about.** Ignorance is not bliss. Security is critical to our personal and national economic health, and we must accept that we can't count on anyone else to rescue us.

5.) **Education is the strongest tool we have for fighting cybercrime.** Motivation doesn't exist without an understanding of the problems to be solved. The only way to overcome sophisticated online con games is by learning to distrust Internet strangers. Dating websites still are not doing enough to warn people or weed out the members who are frauds. Most parents tell their children never to get into a car with a stranger, but too many parents neglect to apply similar rules to online friendships. Appendix H has resources with age-appropriate material (including games and videos) for every child you care about.

Whether your personal involvement with cybercrime is as a career choice, a sideline, a position assisting a nonprofit, or simply a commitment to shore up your own Internet security software and practices, cyber safety is an ever-changing arena with no end of fascinating challenges to sidestep or solve[4]. It's a field where we can help others avoid danger by simply having a conversation. And if you've made it this far you are well-equipped to be part of the solution!

In terms of staying current, I'll be providing updates to the rules, suggestions, and examples in this book every 18 months or so. You can register for notification about updates at my website: www.cjonsecurity.com or www.cynthiajames.com. Thanks for reading and I sincerely hope it has been helpful.

---

4 You will find a wealth of the latest information about jobs – worldwide, which is useful if you'd consider a change of scene – in IT and security at: http://www.theregister.co.uk/jobs/

APPENDIXES A-I

APPENDIX A

The Super Seven Rules for Banking Online

The ideal time to conduct online banking is when you can be sure there are no active infections on your computer. Anti-virus software sends anti-virus updates multiple times a day, and you will want the antivirus software you use to be absolutely current. So, the more time that passes between visiting a website, opening new files, and conducting online banking, the better off you are. Ideally, you will close all your Web pages, ensure that your antivirus is updated, go for a walk, and then do your online banking.

Thus, the only time you should log onto a website connected to your money (banks, credit card companies, investment groups, 401K, etc.) is when you have:

1. Been connected to the internet long enough for your anti-malware to receive its latest anti-cybercrime fixes. (This should happen automatically but open your anti-malware software and check the date and time it last updated. If you need help on how to do this, visit the manufacturer's website.)

2. Opened NO websites in the previous few hours (not even news).

3. Opened NO files in the previous few hours that were emailed to you or downloaded from any instant messaging service or USB stick.

4. Used your very toughest password or passphrase for these accounts – the ones with sensitive or financial data.

5. Never selected the choice which is offered upon login: "remember this computer" or allowed the site to auto-fill your credentials (change this if necessary).

6. Signed up for all the available extra security layers that are available. Most banking websites will now provide additional options such as one additional step of validation.

7. Ensured the link you are logging into is secure. The bank's URL should include an "s" after http so that it reads: https:// (etc.).

Note: Banks now also provide links to additional cybersecurity resources such as information about their email guidelines (to help customers avoid being "phished").[1]

ADDITIONAL BANKING TIPS

8. Any ATM card machine could have a "skimmer" attached to it. Skimmers can detect your card numbers and, when they are combined with your password, your funds can be stolen. Thus:

---

1 See Glossary for a definition.

a. Whenever possible, don't use ATMs that are not attached directly to the bank. It is less likely that bank ATMs will be compromised (but occasionally it still happens).

b. Conceal the pin number you enter. Thieves often mount a web camera with a view of the key pad. They can't crack into your account without a password.

9. Check your credit card statements and bank accounts once a month for any unusual charges, especially small ones. Most banks will reverse losses within 30 days and some will extend that period. If you don't have the time or the interest in checking statements, consider paying someone else to do it for you at least once a quarter. Cybercriminals make millions off of small charges, which people don't notice.

APPENDIX B

Tips for Password Management

We are under constant pressure from the internet universe to produce new login names and passwords. Many sites now won't allow people to post comments without logging in. The easiest method is to create a single user name-login pair and use it everywhere. The problem with this approach is that if we provide the same login name and password for a social website as we do to conduct online banking, and thieves compromise the social website, they now have the ability to access our bank accounts. Stealing login-password pairs and trying them at multiple bank sites is a process which is easily automated by cyber criminals.

What's the alternative? Passwords that are complex and differ for each website provide the ideal level of security. Unfortunately, few of us are able remember so many complex passwords easily. So, like most security choices, we must strike a balance between security and our own comfort and convenience. A good compromise is to select a set of passwords – three is a good number – and use them selectively.

Also, as suggested in Chapter 9, write down your passwords! The old rule of security – which is still repeated by some security authorities – was to never write a password down. But that rule was created during a time when no one could imagine that someday we would need passwords to check our children's grades or that we might need four different passwords just to interact with different sections our company's website. If you don't record your passwords somewhere, you are likely to compromise your security by not making them strong enough. Or, you will waste oodles of time retrieving and resetting them. Many sites such as banks and utility companies won't allow a reset except when preceded by a phone call to customer service. And it's rare that their customer service is available 24/ 7.

Chapter 5 includes eleven rules for Resizing Your Internet Boot Print. Rules 9, 10 and 11 are critical for password safety. Here are some expanded examples:

1. Keep passwords linked with the websites they are used for in a convenient place, but be as cryptic as possible, especially if you keep them in a software file.

   a. If you already know, for example, that you're using the word "ostrich" with the last letter knocked off but you use two different sequences of numbers at the end, one of them being 533, you can write it as: o——5-. Or write, "Joey's favorite animal in second grade (the ostrich)."

   b. There will also be times you need to add a special character. So figure out what that should be and then your list will include o——5-(spec character).

   c. You can also name the number sequences with something which makes sense to only you like "street address in Ohio" or "day we brought home Fido." It is most ideal to use a fact you know that others do not.

2. In the examples above, "ostric533" is your easy password because you think ostriches are cool and 533 was the model of your first car. Your second level of password could then be "ostric533@" just because you like the @ symbol, and your third level of password (for just one or two banks) would be: "Ostric533@^" because you like carrots. If these are the only three passwords you use, you can refer to them as Big Circle (least trusted sites), Medium Circle, and Small Circle (most important sites) passwords.

3. Use your toughest passwords or phrases for the sites that have the most important information about you (health and banking). Don't forget to change your password to something more challenging if you decide to add more personal data to a site. For example if you are using free services but later decide to purchase something or become a subscriber (and add shipping address or billing information).

4. If longer passwords are accepted, use passphrases, the safety of which is discussed in Chapter 9 (why MyLazyDogRex is better than H7%doss!). If the website won't accept the passphrase, at least try not to use complete words which are in the dictionary (there are automatic password crackers which check for every dictionary word). One recent security innovation is that these days many websites will indicate the strength of your password choice. Pay attention to this information where it is offered (where available, it will show up on a website next to your password entry) and select a strong one.

5. If you use a system (for instance at work) requiring you to change passwords every so often, rotate

them. Figure out what the system tolerance is for remembering passwords. Often, the systems won't allow you to use the password you used before the current one, so you can't toggle back and forth. But, you may be able to rotate between three different passwords, or four. In which case, try using the variations in the examples above. Or use peacock and parrot to rotate in with ostrich, using the same rules for dropping the last letter and adding a number.

6. Try not to use open-access public wifi (a wireless network with no password required or for which the password is available to everyone). Or, if you must, at least use it infrequently. Don't conduct online banking from any place other than a secure wireless network.

7. Make sure your router at home requires a password. Many people today use the lengthy model number on the box, but anything long and unique works.

8. Don't share passwords with others in the family (they may share them with non-family members). Ensure that your kids know better than to **ever** give passwords to friends. **Friends don't ask friends for passwords!** Help your family members appreciate that they shouldn't want to know passwords either: if a friend's account is hijacked and used for cyberbullying, it's better not to be on the list of suspects.

APPENDIX C

Six Ways to Avoid Identity Theft

1. Never give out private information over the phone no matter who the caller says they are and do talk to all other household members about this. Callers asking for information such as social security numbers, birth dates, access to computers, etc. may claim they are with:

    a. A company offering computer security (a recent scam as of early 2013 are callers claiming to be from Microsoft support!).

    b. Law enforcement.

    c. A financial institution.

    d. The staff of a sweepstakes, lottery or other contest (which you did not enter but surprisingly have won!)

2. Never provide personal information to a website an email connects you to. If you believe the request is legitimate, there are two safer options:

    a. Type the website address into the browser (rather than using the email link). For example, if you believe the email is from Southwest Airlines, go to the Southwest Airlines site to see if there is a section like the one you received via email.

    b. Call the company (bank, airline, hotel) that sent the email and ask if it has any such offer, prize, or warning.

3. If you become aware that your personal details or those of other family members have been posted by someone else on a blog or website, ask that those details be deleted.

ADVANCING TO THE NEXT LEVEL

4. If you'd like to add more complexity, and thereby more security, create an alias for yourself that involves a new piece of "permanent" data such as a different address (post office boxes can now be rented with street address information). You might also claim a different birth date or birthplace for your parents. In this case, if your data is lost to cybercriminals who breach your bank, they will still have trouble stealing your identity.

5. If your ID is stolen, immediately change all your passwords.

6. Some security experts recommend changing passwords every year. How should you safely change passwords? Follow the online banking rules in Appendix A.

APPENDIX D

13 Tips on Device Management and Automatic Security Updates

First, a few rules on basic device management:

1. Ensure that all mobile devices (laptops, cell phones) are password protected. Ideally, they will also have:

   a. Anti-virus

   b. A remote data wipe feature

   c. Data backup (the best kind operates continuously in the background) – having data backup means you can't be extorted by cybercriminals if they are able to remotely lock your hard drive

2. Implement strong passwords for every wireless router you or other household members use. Make sure for example if they regularly use one at school or at a friend's house they know enough to suggest those routers have protected passwords too.

3. Expect anyone who wants to use your personal wireless network to have anti-virus installed and operating on his or her system.

4. Do not conduct online banking or make purchases outside of the home using an unsecured wireless network

APPLYING FIXES TO THE SECURITY HOLES IN YOUR SOFTWARE

5. Check your system for security vulnerabilities to decide which other security updates to patch automatically. Run a system scan at this website: http://secunia.com/vulnerability_scanning/online/

6. Patch often –applying fixes for the security issues that are constantly being discovered in the software already in use on your devices. Find the setting which will automatically do this for you. Enable automatic updating for all household computers.

7. Patch your browser first. Go to http://security. getnetwise.org/tips/updatingiebrowser.php for updating Internet Explorer or select another option if you use a different browser.

8. Patch your Operating Systems next.
   Go to www.getnetwise.org/videotutorials/ → scroll down to: *Security/Tools* → select: *Keep Your Operating System Security Updated With…* (select operating system).

9. Patch Adobe applications as your third step.

10. Patch Java as the fourth step.

WORKING WITH YOUR ANTI-VIRUS (AV) SOFTWARE

11. As often as it occurs to you, ensure your AV is current before opening a web browser.

12. Be patient with your AV; give it time to do what it needs to do such as scanning download or checking out websites.

13. Listen to your AV; it is very wise. When it says "don't go to that website" or "don't open that email, don't!"

APPENDIX E

Seven Easy Ways to Resize Your Internet Boot Print

The size of an Internet Boot Print should be considered for your entire household. If your daughter follows all the rules for online privacy and safety, it doesn't mean she is safe if your son is sharing too much information with the strangers he plays with online. The household internet Boot Print will still be too big. It is also much better if there are only two credit cards regularly used by the family for internet purchases instead of six. **All seven rules for managing this – constraining the amount of information which is on the internet about your family as a whole – are listed in Chapter 5, page 45.** It's an important concept for family members to understand.

Essentially the discussion begins with these two questions:

- How many different organizations have your data? *This is the width of your Internet boot print.*

- How much data do they have and what type of data is it? *This is the depth of your Internet boot print.*

The family goal should be to make this as small as is practical.

APPENDIX F

Estimate Family Members' Vulnerability and Monitor Children

1. Review the following points to determine what rules each family member needs to learn and educate them accordingly.

Questions to help determine rules for household members:
- Which family members have internet devices and what are they?
    - What activities do they engage in?
        - Examples: gaming, shopping, email, texting, homework/research, banking, etc.

- Which kinds of information will help each family member behave better including:
    - Age-relevant stories (examples – see online resources for this in item 7 below)

    - Infections and how they spread between devices

    o Requirements for anti-virus protection on visitors' computers (before they are allowed to connect to the home internet - when in doubt, run a scan)

2. Never open suspicious email. Give your kids an alternative like forwarding it to you for review.[1]

3. Make sure your children understand that they need to inform you as soon as possible if they have any reason to suspect one of their devices has become infected.

4. Turn off geo locator tags (longitude and latitude coordinates) on all smartphones so they don't show up in photos. (Here is a link on how to do this for iphones: http://www.imore.com/daily-tip-turn-gps-geolocation-iphone-photos-protect-privacy and the following link will help you accomplish the same thing for an Android phone: http://android.stackexchange.com/questions/8741/how-do-i-turn-off-geolocation-when-taking-photos. If it doesn't work, call your service provider or go online to find instructions.)

5. Monitor your children's online activities. There are links to some suggested products and services to help you with monitoring in Appendix G.

6. Help kids create their own aliases– maybe when they are gaming, they set a different time zone, city, or

---

1 Note: Most malware is operating system specific (it can only infect the operating system it was programmed to attack), and the majority of infected web links sent through email are meant to harm PC operating systems. So until or unless cybercriminals begin attacking both the operating systems on cell phones and on PCs using the same infected websites (we have no evidence this is occurring now in 2013), one way to check a suspicious link in an email is to open it on your cell phone and see if the site is legitimate. Of course this is only if you are still suspicious after you have checked the URL and it appears legitimate, and presuming your antivirus is up to date and isn't warning you away from the site.

any other data that is shared with other players. Make sure you are in the loop to approve screen names too.

7. Use online education tools to teach kids. No one speaks to kids quite like other kids do. If you really want them to listen, visit together the website of The National Center for Missing and Exploited Children. There are short videos of stories for kids of all ages illustrating what can go wrong when they don't follow internet safety rules: http://www.netsmartz. org/RealLifeStories. The FBI also offers cyber-safety practices for kids too at: http://www.fbi.gov/news/ stories/2012/october/new-cyber-safety-website-for-teachers-students/new-cyber-safety-website-for-teachers-students . There are lots of really great resources for kids these days – see more links in Appendixes F,G, and H.

8. Stay current. Ask your children to help with this. Provide them the list of sites with information about the latest cybercrime scams or safety for children and let them pick something to share with the family.

9. Make sure everyone in the house understands how easy it is to download an infected application, especially from the Google store on an Android device. While Apple controls its application store with regard to security, at present (early 2013) Google Play does a poor job and it's easy for cybercrime writers to place infected versions of games and other applications in the Google store. For younger children, it's best to prohibit all downloads (without your approval); for teens, agree upon a reasonable process to vet applications before downloading. For example, check reviews and ensure the download your teen

wants is of precisely the correct version of software from the correct publisher.

10. Use old-fashioned methods of keeping tabs on kids if you don't have software yet. Scan cell phone bills for unknown numbers and check their online postings at Twitter and on Facebook. Ideally, you will know their phone passwords so you can randomly monitor text messages as well.

Help Your Village Protect Itself

11. Reach out to charity, churches, or other nonprofits you care about. Ask them if they have any cyber-safety training. If/when they say "no", help them by sharing the links in Appendix H and asking them to schedule time for the staff to view it together.

12. Reach out to schools you care about too. Ask them if cybersafety is part of their curriculum (in too many schools it is not). Public schools should be open about their cybersecurity policies.

Last But Not Least

13. And finally, the most important rule of all: Pay someone to set up any of these rules you don't have time to implement. (Or trade them a meal or some other kindness.) See Appendix H for a list of places to find help.

APPENDIX G

Tools and Organizations to Assist Your Efforts

HIRING HELP

If you want to hire someone who will regularly be in your corner technically, I recommend subscribing to the following issue of *Consumer Reports*. It's completely unbiased and you can select exactly the features you are looking for in a tech support organization. Go to: http://news.consumerreports.org/electronics/2010/03/best-and-worst-tech-support-ratings-laptop-desktop-computer-survey-reviews.html.

That said, I personally have used the Geek Squad at Best Buy with success. I like the fact that I can bring it in if I want or have the techs troubleshoot remotely and that I can cover more than one computer in a subscription. Go to: http://www.geeksquad.com/.

It also shouldn't be difficult to find other companies, both locally and nationally, offering technical support. But whatever you do, don't take a company's word for it – there's a scam right now where people call saying they are from Microsoft Support. They aren't! It's a front for a group trying to install malware on your system and steal credit card numbers. So if you can't get a referral from someone you know, be sure to check reviews from reliable reviewing sites.

If you prefer the "hands-on" approach, local computer stores usually have personnel they can send to your home. Another option is to call the career center of a local college and see if they have computer science students who are interested I in this kind of work. As with anything, check their references and rely on your intuition.

You may also have the option of getting help from a friend or an IT person at work. Just beware that these individuals probably get lots of requests for this kind of thing so be kind – make it worth their while in some way (payment, dinner, etc.). Finally, you might reconsider and try to implement these fixes yourself. Excellent new software paired with on-line videos which show you what to do (YouTube) means that correcting computer issues is easier than it ever has been.

TIPS FOR MONITORING CHILDREN

New products or services to help you monitor your children are released every year. I recommend you talk to other parents and see what they are using. If you are just beginning to look, here are some suggestions. Often the setup is free. There are basically three areas you will want to consider: your child or teen's smartphone texting activity, their social website posting activity, and their computer (web browsing, emailing, etc.) activity.

1. uKnowKids - http://www.uknowkids.com/
   uKnowKids "automatically pulls all of your child's Facebook, Twitter, and Instagram activities so you can monitor what your child is doing online quickly and easily. Save time viewing all your child's social activities in one easy to understand dashboard."

2. Minor Monitor - http://www.minormonitor.com/
   Their product description says it all: "Protect your child from online predators, cyberbullying, and other dangers that can happen on Facebook and Twitter. Receive automated parental alerts any time MinorMonitor detects dangerous activity. Monitor your child's messages, activities, friends, and photos in an easy to use Web dashboard. All of this for free."

3. K9 Web Protection - http://www1.k9webprotection.com/
   This product allows parents to limit web browsing.

4. Norton Family - https://onlinefamily.norton.com/familysafety/whyUseNOF.fs
   From Symantec, this product provides reporting of all kids' activities online. Reports can be emailed to you regularly with a summary of websites visited and what your children have searched for.

5. You might try some of these other Products referenced by New York Times online article in June of 2011 (by the way, you don't usually want to risk trying the very first version of any software, let someone else catch the glitches): http://www.nytimes.com/2012/06/26/technology/software-helps-parents-monitor-their-children-online.html?pagewanted=all&_r=0)

Additionally:
- Try checking cell phone bill for unknown numbers
  Numerous tools are available through the National Cyber Security Alliance, a public (U. S. government is involved)-private alliance: Go to: http://www.staysafeonline.org/.

- If your concern is **gaming** and you'd like to check out parental controls, try the following website. It's created by Microsoft so, while they surely want to see kids game more safely, you won't see any recommendations that kids stop altogether. The site contains some good tips for parents of children who play Xbox: http://www.getgamesmart.com/tools/familysettings/. For tips on recognizing online gaming addiction, go to: http://www.techaddiction.ca/teenagers-addicted-to-computer-games.html

APPENDIX H

Newsletters and Other Ways to Stay Informed

THE LATEST SCAMS AND FRAUDS

It's easy to subscribe to newsletters at most of these sites. Try this one: http://www.ikeepsafe.org/cybersafety/phone-scam-targets-security%e2%80%99s-weakest-link-me/ (the link takes you to a blog about one of the most recent scams in 2013) and it is an excellent overall website with lots of great data. The main website has animated videos for young children and a Parent's Guide for Facebook: http://www.ikeepsafe.org/parents/

And don't forget the Federal Bureau of Investigation (FBI) cyberalert blog. It doesn't offer new blogs frequently, but when the FBI puts out a cyberalert, you can bet it's important (and you can subscribe to receive the alerts): www.fbi.gov . Look under the Story Index for Cybercrime.

CYBERSECURITY ONGOING EDUCATION:

The National Cyber Security Alliance is an organization that provides layers and layers of information on cybersafety. There's something here for everyone. It is a "public-private alliance" (the

U. S. government is involved). Go to: http://www.staysafeonline. org/.

PARENTS PURCHASING SMARTPHONES

If you'd like to see how your choices about **Smartphones** compare to what other parents are deciding and what kids are doing with smartphones (plus more tips), go here: https://www. lookout.com/resources/reports/smartphone-family-guide.

There's also a nice guide you can print and give to your child with their first smartphone. The guide, however, is outdated on one piece of information: you can no longer trust that applications downloaded from Google Play are safe. Otherwise, it's a good document.

TO SHARE WITH CHILDREN OF ALL AGES

www.NetSmartz.org is the website for a safety resource from the National Center for Missing and Exploited Children (NCMEC) and Boys & Girls Clubs of America (BGCA) for children aged 5 to 17, parents, guardians, educators, and law enforcement that uses activities to teach Internet safety.

http://www.onguardonline.gov/ is the FTC's main consumer-facing website with lots of great, fresh information.

http://www.webwisekids.org/ has great material for kids (every teenage girl should hear Katie's Story, presented by Katie herself). The site offers fun, interactive simulations based on real-life criminal cases. This is the place to go if you would like to help encourage schools in the area to educate children on cyber safety.

https://www.wiredsafety.org/ - more great stuff for parents to share with kids.

HERE'S A TOOL FROM THE FBI WHICH TEACHES CYBER SAFETY:

http://www.fbi.gov/news/stories/2012/october/new-cyber-safety-website-for-teachers-students/new-cyber-safety-website-for-teachers-students.

APPENDIX I

Glossary

Note: The purpose of the following glossary is to acquaint the nontechnical person with a few cyber-security related terms with which he or she may be unfamiliar. It is not intended to be a comprehensive listing of security terms as that could easily constitute a book in itself.

BACK DOOR

This is an access "doorway" (a figurative opening) integrated into a product by software and hardware designers. These doorways are created for use during product development and testing at customer sites – before the final product is shipped. Their purpose is to allow designers to manipulate or change a product *remotely*. For example, if the code on a copy of beta software accidently crashes a new system, by using a "back door" an IT professional can log in remotely and download fresh code. This provides a quick fix and avoids the necessity of shipping a whole new product. For security reasons, back doors are supposed to be boarded shut when the product is finalized. Sometimes product managers neglect to do this. Usually it is an error in development to leave the door open. However, in very rare cases, companies have been accused of installing back doors so they can spy on customers. Naturally, cybercriminals love to discover backdoors. Sometimes the first time they learn about one is when a company notifies its customers that they exist. As is always the case with security fixes, there will be customers who never install the fix required to close the door.

BOTNET

A network of zombie systems which is managed and controlled by a botherder. Zombies are computers which have been converted – by the application of malicious software – into "bots" without the knowledge of the device owner.

BREACH

To break or penetrate a company's cybersecurity; often, such attacks are successfully executed by cybercriminals. A successful breach doesn't always mean the criminal succeeded in stealing data. Although when a company admits to having "sustained a breach," it can be assumed that they probably lost some data of value to them, whether intellectual property or customer records.

CATFISHING

The practice of pretending to be someone else on a dating or social networking site in order to exploit another person. Commonly catfishers steal photos of other people which they then set up profiles for.

COMPROMISE

The term used in cybercrime circles to refer to a successful attack. If a company has been compromised it means their security has been breached and data has been stolen.

COMPLIANCE

When used in a computing context, this word means the act of complying with or conforming to a rule or set of standards, however, it's usually coupled with the name of a specific standard such as, "We need to prove compliance with GLBA" (a reference to the Gramm-Leach-Bliley Act). Increasingly, businesses are being challenged to prove a certain level of cyber safety awareness or preparedness according to standards set either by the government or industry standard-setting groups. Cyber awareness training can be used to satisfy these requirements.

COOKIES

Short for "magic cookies", these are described in detail in Chapter 5.

DARKNET

In the days of Internet infancy, this was the name used for networks that were separate from ARPANET for security reasons. A darknet is a network that receives information but won't respond to public pings. So it is anonymous; it only communicates with trusted "friends." Re-popularized in the last decade, the term has been used to allow people who living in authoritarian countries to use the internet without being imprisoned. Unfortunately the term has also been used for cybercrime in certain ways, such as to hide the identities of child molesters.

DENIAL OF SERVICE ATTACK (DOS BUT USUALLY CALLED "DISTRIBUTED DENIAL OF SERVICE ATTACK" OR DDOS)

When you try to go to a website and the website is down, you may see a message which says, "service denied". There are basically three goals hackers have when attacking Web servers. They want to:

1.) Break though the server and get into the company the server belongs to (in order to steal data, etc.)

2.) Take whatever data of any value the Web server has on it (security protocol demands that customer data is held off the Web server itself, but not everyone follows that rule)

3.) Overwhelm the Web server with requests to load web pages, to the point where the Web server is not able to process any new requests and thereby "denies service" to everyone. When a news report says that hacktivists "took down" the Justice Department's Web server in retaliation, this is likely what happened. Everyone trying to reach their website will get a notice that the Web page cannot load.

The reason this is called a "Distributed" DOS is because the most efficient way to carry out such an attack is to have many requests launched from many different locations (hence they are distributed). This is an ideal job for a botnet of zombies. Botherders are happy to rent out their botnets for days at a time simply to harangue websites to the point where they fail.

DRIVE-BY DOWNLOAD

Any malware which is installed on a user's system without their knowledge or consent. The term comes from the idea that as a result of merely "driving by" a website, malware can jump onto your system. No clicking necessary. Sometimes it is also used to describe malware which rides along with something legitimate like a software driver.

HONEY POT

A system which is set up to be an attractive (low security but high value) attack target. By setting up lots of these in different parts of the world anti-malware companies can see what cybercriminals are doing. This can help us, the good guys, recognize and defeat viruses before they reach systems we want to protect. It can also provide an early warning system about trends and indicate what intruders are looking for.

IDENTITY THEFT

The unauthorized use of an individual's personal information so as to masquerade as that individual. Identity theft doesn't always have to occur in cyberspace: sometimes card numbers and other details are purchased so criminals can show up at dealerships and buy cars (see Chapter 5 for more details).

LULZ

In computer-ese, the term implies the reason for posting funny, weird, or insensitive material or doing things that might be considered inappropriate. Lulz is a word described variously as "the internet version of LOL" (laugh out loud). Hackers and Hacktivists sometimes describe this as the reason for something they have done.[1]

MALWARE

Short for "malicious software", malware denotes all forms of bad cyber stuff. Years ago, what we most cared about was catching viruses, a very specific type of threat that spreads itself in a specific way. Back then, we called the software that attacks viruses "anti-virus" or AV for short. The old anti-virus software has evolved so that now it fights worms, Trojans, and all kinds of mixed threats, which means it has really become "anti-malware". However, so many people became accustomed to calling their computer protection "anti-virus" and so few people know what "malware" means that we have come to use the terms "anti-virus" and "anti-malware" interchangeably.

---

1 Read more here: http://www.theglobeandmail.com/technology/tech-news/hacking-group-says-they-do-it-for-the-lulz/article556865/

MICROSOFT'S "PATCH TUESDAY"

Patch Tuesday is a name coined by the industry to describe the regularly scheduled day when Microsoft sends out security fixes. The fixes are to address vulnerabilities which have been discovered in their products such as Windows and Explorer. This happens on the second Tuesday of each month. Along with the fixes comes a description of what they are for, including a severity rating. Some other software companies have followed suit so that Adobe now provides updates to their Flash Player product on Patch Tuesdays as well. *Of course when Microsoft issues these updates, they are also providing data to cybercriminals which can be used to infect systems (see Hacker Hal's story in Chapter 3), but there is currently no better method than using public broadcast to communicate with such a large audience.*

PASTEBIN

Synonymous with the company providing it, this mechanism allows people to "paste" data or information that can be retrieved or read by others. Since there's no link between the data and the person who posted it, Pastebin can be used by hackers who want to remain anonymous. They might use Pastebin to "prove" they stole data, or it can even be a way for hacktivists to transfer data to other people anonymously. In some cases hacktivists have used this as a means to communicate with law enforcement regarding cyberpredators or animal cruelty perpetrators. *Of course there are lots of legitimate business and social reasons to use Pastebin also.*[2]

PHISHING

The practice of sending spam that entices users into inputting enough information that their identities can be stolen. The email might say something like, "your bank needs you to contact us immediately" or "click here to claim your prize!" When the user clicks on the link it goes to a website with the correct (albeit often

---

2 http://pastebin.com/

fuzzy) bank logo, and it provides a form you must fill in with all your information. Hundreds of thousands of people fall for this every year. *Of course, no legitimate company ever asks customers for this kind of information over email. If it looks legitimate, the best policy is always to call to verify.*

PRETEXTING

The effort or strategy to conceal something. We use the term "pretexting" when someone does this for the purpose of obtaining information illegally. It is most often used when someone like a private investigator pretends to be someone else. For example, an investigator trying to obtain Mr. Johnson's cell phone records pretends to be Mr. Johnson. A high-profile case of this involved the board of Hewlett Packard (HP). In an effort to discover the person who was leaking information, HP executives hired investigators to spy on other board members, reporters, and their families. It caused a big scandal – since pretexting is illegal.[3]

SINKHOLE

A "sinkhole" is a popular method used by anti-malware companies to determine how many zombies there are in a given botnet. The easiest way to explain how sinkholes work is that the good guys hijack the address used by the botherder for long enough to count how many computers try to say "hello" to their botherder (leader).

SOCIAL ENGINEERING

Simplistically defined, the phrase, "social engineering" means "manipulating people." The term was invented by geeks to glorify the sorts of techniques that salespeople and con men have used for millennia to achieve their goals. Social engineering encompasses

---

3 But all is well that ends well. After it was all over, there was some financial benefit in it for California district attorneys and local cybercrime enforcement when HP agreed to pay a multi-million dollar fine. Go to: http://www.wired.com/wiredenterprise/2012/12/pretexting-california/.

everything from sending an email that entices the receiver to "click here and see what you won!" to the pretext of being the CEO's daughter to get the password to the customer database.

TWO FACTOR AUTHENTICATION

This is very much like showing "two forms of ID" over the internet. Single factor authentication is when the only requirement for entering a website is a password and user name combination. Two factor authentication is when a site asks you to verify yourself using a second method as well. For example, after logging in, some sites ask you to also answer a security question. Or the site might send a text message to the cell phone on file with a code number which must be input in order to continue. There are many ways to double-validate yourself, and they differ in terms of how convenient and effective they are. Whenever there are a series of high-profile hacks, such as when the twitter accounts of Burger King and Jeep were hacked in early 2013, people begin asking: why isn't that service using two-factor identity validation? Another common example of two factor authentication is when your bank has registered the cell phone or PC you most often use for online banking (via a cookie the bank has placed on the device earlier), but you try to connect from a new device. In that case, you may be asked additional security questions to confirm it is you.

VULNERABILITY

Security holes in a product are considered vulnerabilities. A security hole could also be considered a subset of software bugs (mistakes in the code) but we like the term "hole" better because we think of malicious software as "crawling in." Also, a software program with lots of security holes can still be a very high-functioning product. Just because the developer didn't think of every awful or crazy thing cybercriminals would try in order to bypass security doesn't mean the application itself is bad. Cybercriminals wouldn't try so hard if it wasn't a popular application; they rarely try to break applications unless the applications have spread across at least millions of devices. Once an application has reached critical mass (the way Windows or Java have – Java is now on over *three billion* devices), it becomes an irresistible target.

Another way to use the word is as a descriptor of "how exposed we are to harm" as in the phrase, "Acme is a company who provides vulnerability assessments for small businesses."

WATERING HOLE

This term describes a site which is often visited by companies a cybercriminal is targeting. In order to infect the targets, cybercriminals will "poison the well" – infect the website – with a malware infection. For example, suppose s/he intends to infect defense contractors. The challenge with this will be that defense contractors tend to have very strong security measures in place. Thus, it is easier to find a website with lower security standards which the contractors visit frequently.

ZOMBIE

When your system no longer has a mind of its own, it has become a zombie. It will follow the instructions of "command and control", otherwise known as the botherder, and may do things such as send spam while you are sleeping or hijack your identity. The only fix is to de-infect by installing anti-malware. *Of course the malware which caused the infection will resist attempts to do this and it may require wiping the hard drive to get it done.*

About the Author

Cynthia James is a career professional in high tech with over 25 years of experience. She has spent the last seven years exclusively focused in the area of cybersecurity. She possesses one of the world's most rigorous security certifications, the CISSP (Certified Information Systems Security Professional) that requires knowledge of best security practices within 10 different areas, including physical security and software development and encryption. In her job with Kaspersky Lab, a multinational computer security company, Cynthia speaks, writes, and teaches extensively about cybercrime. She wrote *Stop Cybercrime from Ruining YOUR Life* to address the gap between the complexities of the cybercrime environment and the average person's need for simplified information and basic principles of protection.

Cynthia lives in Silicon Valley with her two children and their various pets. She has a degree in Economics from University of California and is also a student of Russian, a pilot, and a trail runner.

www.ingramcontent.com/pod-product-compliance
Lightning Source LLC
LaVergne TN
LVHW051630080426
835511LV00016B/2272